Art Class

Art Class

*A beginner's complete guide
to painting and drawing*

Edited by

KEN HOWARD

WATSON-GUPTILL PUBLICATIONS/NEW YORK

First published in 1989 in the United States by
Watson–Guptill Publications, a division of Billboard Publications, Inc.,
1515 Broadway, New York, New York 10036.

Conceived and produced by
Swallow Publishing Ltd,
260 Pentonville Road, London N1 9JY

Library of Congress Cataloging in Publication Data
Art class.
    Originally published as 4 separate vol.: London:
Bloomsbury Pub., 1988.
    Includes index.
    1. Art — Technique.   2. Composition (Art)
3. Perspective. I. Howard, Ken, 1932-
N7430.A6965   1989   751.4   89-5788
ISBN 0-8230-0256-X

Note: Throughout this book, American terms are signalled in
parentheses after their British equivalents the first time in
each chapter they occur. In paper sizes, the nearest
available stock size is given. In frame and artwork measurement, height
always precedes width.

Printed in Singapore
First printing, 1989
1 2 3 4 5/93 92 91 90 89

Contents

Foreword by Ken Howard

'I wish I could do that.'
This is probably the most common exclamation by anyone watching an artist at work. Wishing will not achieve it but practice might. It is my belief that most people can paint and draw if they really want to and if they receive some form of guidance. When we are at school it is taken for granted that everyone can be taught to write but not necessarily that they will write great poetry or prose. I believe that everyone can be taught to paint and draw for their own pleasure, but that does not mean that they will produce masterpieces. Great artists are born, but how can we know whether we are an artist or not until we have learned to paint?

Ken Howard 'Spring Light Mousehole' 1200 × 1000mm (48 × 40in.). Oil.

Ken Howard 'Summer Evening '89'
200 × 300mm (8 × 12in.).
Watercolour.

In the past, artists learned by going to work in a master's studio. There they would start by cleaning the artist's palette and doing odd jobs around the studio, then begin to learn about materials and methods, and eventually be trusted to lay in the foundation of the master's work. Finally, they would set out on their own towards excellence and individuality.

At the end of the nineteenth century, with the advent of the photograph and decline in commissioned works, the artist's studio was replaced by the art schools. Through foundation and degree courses, students again learned the basics of materials and methods and were encouraged to develop their imaginations so that when they graduated they could start on the long road to achieving excellence in their chosen field.

Today, through the social reforms that have cut working hours and given people the time and money to pursue their passions, there are many thousands of amateur artists who are looking for an equivalent of the master's studio or the art school in order to learn the basic skills of their avocation. In the past, amateurs – the 'lovers of art' – pursued excellence with as much dedication as professionals; the only difference was that they did not earn their living from art. Just as in sport and other fields, this did not mean that the amateur did not strive for perfection in what he or she was practising.

Art Class is a book geared specifically to the requirements of the amateur artist. Its aim is to give the would-be painter training equal to what might be learned as an artist's apprentice or in an art school foundation course. The first three sections, covering drawing, working in watercolour and working in oils, are technique-based to help you to acquire first the basic, then the more advanced, skills you need to start working in a particular medium; the final section deals with composition and perspective, outlining the theory and principles which you should understand and then apply in order to produce pleasing and technically adept works of art. The book is full of sound practical advice, and suggests exercises and projects like those the students on foundation courses are given to ensure their clear understanding of a subject. All the contributing writers, as well as being highly regarded professional artists, have at some time in their careers been involved in teaching in art schools; indeed I have had the pleasure of teaching with them on one of the most prestigious foundation courses at a leading London art school.

Drawing and painting involve the heart, the hand and the head. The heart moves us to paint. The hand we can only develop through practice, and this book at all times stresses the importance of practice. The head involves understanding what goes into the process of making a painting and this book covers these main elements: drawing, tone, and colour, as well as composition, which is the most important of all.

Drawing I consider to be the basis of all painting. There have been many draughtsmen who could not paint, but I have never discovered a painter who could not draw. Drawing, like writing, has a grammar. Just as writing is made up of letters, words, sentences and paragraphs, drawing is made up of marks, lines, shapes and tones. When we are young, we learn to write through practice and thus we develop our own handwriting. Drawing too demands practice, and through that we develop our own style.

Jason Bowyer's contribution to this book is a coherent introduction to the elements of drawing. Starting with advice on materials and organizing a work space, he considers the most basic questions such as whether you should stand or sit to work and how to make marks with pencils, ink and charcoal. He then takes us step by step through projects in various media and opens our eyes to ideas for subjects to draw. His advice is equally appropriate whether you want to draw for its own sake, using the techniques described to produce finished works, or improve your drawing skills in order to make more successful paintings.

Charles Bartlett, who contributes the section on Starting in Watercolour, is a man of great experience in both the practice and teaching of watercolour painting, and is President of the Royal Society of Painters in Water-Colours. His own watercolours are full of experiment and verve and in this book he encourages the same lively approach. He describes a whole variety of materials, based on his experience over many years. He explores watercolour techniques, beginning with the most traditional methods of working with transparent washes and working wet into wet, followed by more varied and adventurous approaches. Although he cannot actually have you sit and watch him work, he does the next best thing and takes you step by step through projects, explaining the development of a painting clearly and concisely.

Jason Bowyer 'Jimmy's Boat'
175 × 228mm (6¾ × 9in.).
Charcoal.

Charles Bartlett 'Reeds'
426 × 575mm (17 × 23in.).
Watercolour.

Roy Rodgers' contribution, Starting in Oils, is full of helpful instruction and knowledge about the process of oil painting of which he has a wide experience as an exhibiting painter, as a designer for film and television, and as a teacher of many years' experience. He shows oil paint to be a liberating medium, full of varied possibilities and not in the least hidebound by tradition or technique.

The most important element of learning to paint is that you must love to do it. That does not mean that it will not be difficult and that you may want to give up, but once you have been bitten, you will always try again. As you practise you will get better, and as you get better you will want to practise more, and as you practise more you will get even better.

A very common mistake among people who are beginning to paint is to believe that having done a subject once, that is enough. This of course is quite wrong. If you look at works by Masters, you will see that they sometimes pursued the same idea for years. When using a book like *Art Class* there is the danger that having worked through a project once, you may feel it is done or, worse still, that you have failed to achieve a result that satisfies you. In order to achieve a good result it is necessary to do the projects many times, and each time you will find you get nearer to the desired aim.

The most difficult, but very necessary, element to grasp in drawing and painting is composition, or the arranging of the parts into a whole. In painting a landscape, for example, it is relatively easy to draw a building, a tree or a fence, but fitting them together coherently is the hard part, and it is here of

Roy Rodgers 'Grass in Sunlight'
1010 × 760mm (40 × 30½in.).
Oil.

course that the element of perspective clearly enters into the problem. In the last section of the book, Bill Ward, an experienced painter, etcher and illustrator, offers a thorough explanation of the principles of composition and perspective to give anyone who is interested in a serious understanding of picture making a solid base on which to practise and build.

At one time, every art student had to learn the fundamentals of perspective. It was never an easy process and yet it was a discipline which every student came to understand. The fundamentals of composition were also taught, as was an understanding of the principles of the golden section or divine proportion. What we learned with time was that through practice these disciplines could eventually become intuitive.

By understanding the golden section it becomes part of our sensibility; by understanding perspective it is eventually part of our way of seeing, which we can use, discard, or bend according to our needs.

I have enjoyed editing the contributions of these four gifted artists and teachers to *Art Class* enormously. For me, the experience was one of rediscovery. We learn things consciously when we begin to draw and paint and eventually they become part of our subconscious, and we use them intuitively. To have these lessons brought back to the surface by this book has indeed been an exciting revelation, sometimes a re-evaluation.

Read this book, enter into its enthusiasms, practise what is given and, basing your efforts on its sound foundation, enjoy drawing and painting as they are meant to be enjoyed.

T. W. Ward 'Hauled Out for a Polish' 624 × 477mm (25 × 19in.). Gouache.

PART ONE

Starting Drawing

Introduction

Drawing is the simplest and oldest art form. Drawn images are created by adults and children of all ages, in order to express feelings, communicate ideas to others, or simply for pleasure and the exhilaration of the act. Drawing is practised using different methods and materials, and in various forms in every culture and society throughout the world. Whatever the tools, whether pencil, charcoal, ink or pastel, all drawings are executed either in line or tone (or both). Line drawings are made purely in lines, whereas tone involves shading and degrees of light and dark.

The ability to draw and communicate through drawn marks is not a talent possessed by only a few people, but can be embraced by everyone with a little effort. This section will provide you with only a fraction of the enormous vocabulary of techniques and materials used in drawing. It is not intended to be definitive, but will show you one way to approach your first steps in drawing. At the heart of the information lies the belief that the person starting to draw must begin by observing the world around them before embarking on problems of expression.

". . . and every day I am more convinced that people who do not first wrestle with nature never succeed."
Van Gogh, Nuenan, January 1885

This is how I started to draw myself. Seated at the kitchen table, working in pencil from observation, I learned the rudiments of measurement and simply got on with it. One of my earliest subject matters was a mound of potato peelings. It became an exciting wriggling pattern once I started to draw and observe.

". . . Now hardly a day passes that I do not make something. As practice makes perfect, I cannot but make progress; each drawing one makes, each study one paints, is a step forward."
Van Gogh, Denthe, October 1883

For this reason, this section is built around exercises which are designed to develop your visual vocabulary of marks, lines and tone. I hope you will gain confidence through them and be unafraid to make mistakes as you progress. The simple exercises will begin to develop your awareness of space around you and the scale of objects; you will then be able to learn how to work from observation and to produce drawings exploring measurement and proportion.

Vincent van Gogh 'La Crau from Mont Majour' (detail) 480 × 608mm (19¼ × 24⅓in.). Van Gogh achieves a unified and peaceful composition using short, staccato lines and dots in ink. He creates a vast panorama with varying tonal marks that recede from the denser marks of the foreground to the vague suggestion of the horizon line.

Peter Paul Rubens 'Cows' (detail) 340 × 522mm (13⅜ × 20½in.). This drawing uses a combination of brown sepia ink and dip pen. The delicate, flowing lines of the dip pen capture the movement of the cows. The small sketches around the main study emphasize Rubens' interest in analysing the changing forms of the cow.

Materials, equipment and the workspace

You need only spend a little money to buy the simple materials needed to start drawing. There is, in fact, a wide variety of materials and equipment available, all of them with their uses, but only a selection of them is necessary for the beginner. To enable you to acquire equipment gradually, a list of materials is given wherever specific drawing projects are prescribed in this section, and you can just buy what you need for that type of drawing if you do not already have it.

The marks produced by different drawing media that are illustrated here are not to be taken as being definitive; they are merely examples of how to achieve various effects. It is important to develop your own way of working.

A selection of equipment from the kit recommended for the drawing exercises and projects.

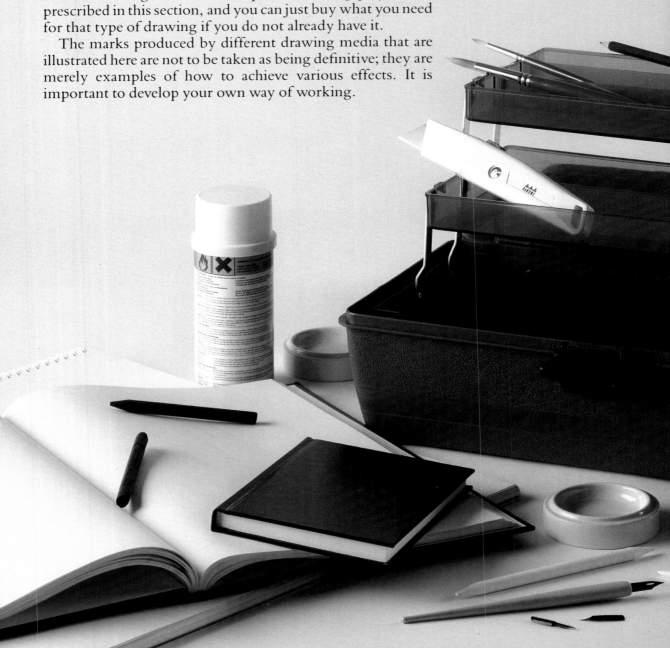

Recommended kit

The following pieces of equipment are easily available from art shops and hardware stores. The materials can be bought fairly inexpensively, especially if you shop around. With these you will be able to do the exercises and projects given in this section.

a plywood drawing board measuring 55 × 50cm (22 × 20in.)
white cartridge (drawing) paper in different sizes
an A3 (18 × 12in.) sketchpad of cartridge paper
a hardback sketchbook
2B, 4B and 6B pencils
a box of thick charcoal sticks, a few pieces of compressed charcoal and a soft charcoal pencil
a metal dip pen with a variety of nibs
a reed or bamboo pen
three nylon brushes
a plastic eraser
a bottle of Indian (India) ink (waterproof)
a white oil crayon
a tube of white gouache
a plastic or ceramic stacking palette (cabinet nest)
a sharp craft knife such as a Stanley knife
a roll of masking tape or adhesive tape
a roll of gummed tape
rubber-based adhesive
a can of spray fixative
a metal ruler
a storage box

Basic equipment

Pencils

Pencil is a very popular medium due to its wide variety of uses in line drawing and tonal work, and its portability, which makes it ideal for impromptu sketching. It is probably also the tool that most readily comes to mind when people think of drawing. In artistic terms, however, the pencil is a relative newcomer, being invented by a Frenchman, Nicolas Jacques Conté, in 1795.

The central part of the pencil is made from carbon and clay. This part varies from hard to soft, and all pencils are graded accordingly. The harder ones range from H to 8H; the higher the number, the harder they are. Likewise with the soft ones, which start at B and go up to 8B. HB pencils are of intermediate hardness.

Hard pencils make a fine, sharp line, soft ones a dark line that can be sharp or soft, and are therefore more versatile in their use. Sharpened they make fine lines, rounded they produce soft, thick ones, and they are also useful in producing areas of tone. A good basic group to have is a range from soft to very soft, say a 2B, 4B and 6B.

Charcoal

Charcoal is the oldest drawing medium, and its origins probably go back to when the first cave-dweller picked a piece of burnt wood from the fire and started to make marks with it. When used for drawing it is shaped into sticks, or is in the form of a pencil. Like pencil, it can vary in hardness. Charcoal is often used to create tonal drawings because of the ease with which it can cover large areas.

Three types of charcoal are available:

Stick charcoal   This comes in a variety of thicknesses and lengths. Sometimes the sticks are sold separately but generally they are in a box containing 10 or 20. The thinnest sticks are usually used for line drawing. The thicker sticks are suitable for making tonal areas but can also be used for making a variety of lines.

Compressed charcoal   This comes in short sticks, and has a darker tone than stick charcoal. It is difficult to make a thin line with a piece of compressed charcoal unless it is sharpened but is very useful when you need a deep black tone to heighten the contrast in a stick charcoal drawing.

Charcoal pencils   These are graded extra soft, soft, medium and hard. They are used for line drawings and work well in quick sketchbook drawings. They are valuable when you need a sharp line to define the shape in a tonal stick charcoal drawing.

Paper

Paper is available in a range of sizes and surfaces. It is made from various combinations of wood fibre, flax, hemp and cotton. Sizes are identified by a coding system. The largest size ordinarily available is A1, measuring 841 × 594mm (or about 36 × 24in.), the smallest A5, measuring 210 × 148mm (about 8½ × 5½in.).

The surface of paper can vary. Hand-made paper may have a textured surface or a smooth finish. A mass-produced paper will have a smooth finish. Papers made with a rag content make by far the most stable surface for your drawings, but can be prohibitively expensive. A simple A3 sketchpad of mass-produced cartridge (drawing) paper, measuring 420 × 297mm (18 × 12in.), will be adequate for the beginner.

Pens

Pens have been used for drawing since the early Middle Ages. They are commonly used by designers and draughtsmen, as well as by fine artists. Ink gives a darker, firmer line than pencil, the thickness of the line being determined by the fineness of the nib.

Reed and bamboo pens   Soft-wooded pens do not have any kind of canal or storage chamber to hold ink in, and therefore have to be dipped into ink frequently. The line that they create is usually rich and thick, varying according to the way the nib is cut.

Quill pens   The quill feathers of birds, sharpened to a point, are often used for drawing with. Only naturally discarded feathers are suitable as they have to have attained sufficient maturity. The line created is elegant, and this makes them popular for calligraphy.

Metal dip pens   The metal nibs which you insert into wooden or plastic pen holders come in varying thicknesses. These nibs retain a certain amount of ink, and so they do not have to be dipped too often.

Reservoir and fountain pens   The reservoir pen has interchangeable nibs and is used by graphic and commercial artists. The ordinary fountain pen does not produce the versatility of line that is useful for the beginner to explore, and so is not generally recommended.

Initially you need only a wooden pen holder and a range of different thicknesses of nib. It would be useful, however, to have either a reed or bamboo pen.

Brushes

A pen and brushes that can be used together can create exciting marks and are especially valuable in doing tone work. Your basic drawing equipment should include brushes made from nylon fibre or nylon with a mix of sable. A size 2 round-ended, a size 7 round-ended and a size 8 flat-ended are a good basic set to begin with. With these brushes you will be able to work in line as well as create tonal washes for your drawings.

Ink

The first inks were made from candle soot and gum water in ancient China; they came in a solid form and were mixed with water. The Chinese used them for writing and drawing. Modern drawing inks like Indian ink (more often known as India ink in the USA) are made from gas black in aqueous adhesive; the addition of shellac soap makes them waterproof. Indian ink is excellent for drawing with, particularly for beginners because it is readily available and easy to manipulate.

Drawing board

It is essential to have a drawing board as this gives you a firm surface to work on. The best type of drawing board for the beginner is one made of light plywood measuring approximately 55 × 50cm (22 × 20in.). Your local timber merchant can cut you a board to size.

Erasers

The first erasers were made of either soft leather or freshly baked bread, but the discovery of rubber and the development of plastic have resulted in these crude forms of erasers dying out. Plastic erasers are excellent for pencil and charcoal. However, erasing ink is difficult, and commercial erasers cannot cope. The best way is to scrape the surface of the paper lightly with a sharp craft knife or a scalpel (X-acto knife). To get a sharp edge to a plastic eraser, cut with a sharp knife periodically.

Fibrous paper sticks commonly known as paper stumps (stomps) and properly called tortillon, are useful for spreading charcoal.

Other equipment

Charcoal and soft pencil will smudge quite easily if not treated, so fixatives are available which make dry mediums more permanent on paper. They come in the form of spray-on liquid. Instructions for use are always given on the side of the container and should be followed carefully.

Artists' oil crayons are impervious to water and are used when working in mixed media.

Cutting tools are essential for sharpening pencils and for cutting paper or card. A sharp craft knife is ideal for both of these tasks.

Drawing pins and masking tape are needed to attach paper to a drawing board or to put newly made drawings on the wall.

A metal ruler at least 30cm (12in.) in length is helpful both for cutting card and for marking out areas to draw in.

Finally, a storage box such as an old tool box or a plastic art bin is useful for organizing your equipment and keeping it together.

Recommended furniture (from left to right): a table, drawing board, chair, box easel, sketching easel, and radial easel.

22

Furniture

Table   You are going to need a table both to work at and to rest your drawing board against. It should be at a comfortable height.

Chair   A good kitchen chair without arms and giving your back support is essential for drawing in a seated position. A stool placed beside you is often useful for materials.

Easel   An easel is not essential when you are starting to learn to draw providing that you have a drawing board. If, however, you do have one it will give you a vertical surface to work on. You can either sit comfortably at arm's length from your board or stand to draw if your subject matter is on a shelf. The benefit of standing is that you can view your work from a varying distance more easily. This gives the eye a chance to scan the whole of the drawing. The proportions will become clearer to you: the size and scale of objects in relation to one another can be understood and altered.

There are three varieties of easel:

Radial easel   Commonly used in art schools, it is a large piece of equipment and hence not suitable for the average home.

Sketching easel   A collapsible easel that can easily be stored in a cupboard.

Box easel   A collapsible easel that folds down into and around the main box support. A useful, more stable version of the sketching easel.

Setting up

A little effort given to setting up will give you the chance to use your precious time more profitably. Looking for a missing pencil or eraser is frustrating and destroys your creative urge, leaving you exasperated and in no frame of mind to concentrate. It is best, therefore, to have everything you will need to hand when you start.

If you don't have anywhere you can use as a small permanent workspace, store all your materials in an art bin or tool box. Keep them in separate compartments so that you can find them without having to rummage around.

Organizing a small space

If possible, use part of a room permanently as your art area. An hour or two spent initially in arranging furniture, obtaining materials and organizing lighting will ultimately give you more time to draw. In deciding upon a desirable space, consider these points:

Light   It's important to choose somewhere with good, constant light – a space near a window, not a badly lit corner. You may want to work at night, so also make sure that you have sufficient artificial light to avoid straining your eyes.

Noise   Obviously, it's difficult to concentrate with constant noise and people moving around. Try to find a place where you will not be continually disturbed.

Heat   You may need to use your space in the winter for drawing. Find a place that has adequate heating. It's not advisable to have your space right next to a radiator as the heat would adversely affect the paper and art materials.

Sitting and standing to draw

Standing   Work at arm's length; it is impossible to get the proportions right if you work too close to the paper. It is a good idea to have a stool close by so that you can sit down occasionally to rest your legs, while you contemplate your work from a different position.

The author standing to draw.

Sitting   Most people find that sitting is more comfortable for drawing than standing, and certainly with most drawings there is no reason why you should not sit down. The important thing is that you have a good view of both your subject matter and your drawing board.

Choose a chair that gives your back support, then lean your drawing board on the edge of the table at an angle of 45 degrees so that it can rest easily on your lap. Try not to slouch or lean on your board as you draw. It is important to move away from your board at intervals of about 30 minutes so as to view your work from a distance. This enables you to check that the proportions are correct and that the tones work together as a whole. But do not move your chair or your subject, as when you sit down again you need to see what you are drawing from the same angle and position.

The author sitting to draw.

Stretching paper

When you come to draw with washes (pen and ink), you will need to be able to stretch the paper first. This is a way of wetting the paper and letting it dry so as to prevent it from wrinkling as the ink dries. The procedure is not as difficult as you might think and can be learned quickly.

If you are going to use your actual drawing board, keep to one side only, so you can preserve the other as a clean drawing surface. If you prefer, keep a separate board just for stretching paper. This will enable you to prepare paper and continue with other drawings at the same time.

First, place the paper in the centre of the board. Measure four lengths of gummed tape for the sides of the paper, making them slightly longer so they will overlap at the corners. Put these aside.

Then, gently dampen the surface of the paper with a sponge, turn the paper over, and repeat the process. Make sure the sponge is not too saturated with water – squeeze it out lightly before you start. Take care not to rub too hard as you could damage the surface of the paper.

Now fix the paper to the board. Run a strip of gummed tape under the tap (or through a dish of water) and lightly pull it through your fingers and thumb to get rid of the excess water (but do not remove the gum from the surface). Place the strip of tape along one edge of the paper so that half the width is over the paper and half is over the board. Repeat with the remaining strips of tape.

As you fix the tape, wipe along its edges with the sponge to absorb any excess water, and to make sure it is flat and has stuck all the way round. Do the same over the surface of the paper but just dabbing gently.

Allow the paper to dry at room temperature. Keep the board flat so the paper can dry evenly. Do not attempt to speed up the process by using a fan heater or by putting it beside a radiator as this would probably make the paper tear or buckle. When the paper is dry, it should be completely flat and ready to use.

HOW TO STRETCH PAPER

After placing your paper in the centre of the board, measure the four lengths of gummed tape to be slightly longer than each side of the paper (in order to overlap at the corners).

Using a sponge that is wet but not saturated, dampen the surface of the paper evenly to relax the fibres in the paper. Then turn the paper over and dampen the other side.

Wet the gummed tape by either running it under a tap or through a dish of water, gently taking off the excess water with your fingers and thumb.

Having fixed the gummed tape along the four edges of the paper in such a way that half of the tape width is over the board, wipe off any excess water with the sponge.

Basic line techniques

Line drawing is simply the drawing of shapes with lines only, without any shading or tone. It is the most basic form of drawing, and as such is the foundation for every other technique. However, this does not mean that it is somehow inferior to other forms of art, for line on its own provides enormous scope. Look at the different types of line that are all around you: the sharp, straight line of a window, the curved lines of a cup, or the crinkly edge of a fern, for example.

The initial step when approaching drawing for the first time is to investigate the varieties of line made by the different media so as to become familiar with them before working from observation.

You will need
☐ a drawing board
☐ A3 (18 × 12in.) paper
☐ 2B, 4B and 6B pencils
☐ a dip pen, nibs and ink
☐ brushes
☐ a plastic eraser
☐ a ruler
☐ masking tape
☐ a sharp craft knife
☐ a stacking palette (cabinet nest)
☐ a container of water

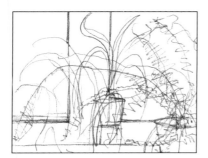 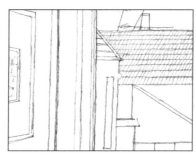

Far left: The sharp, straight lines of the window frame make a stark contrast to the zig-zagging, curling plant leaves.
Left: View through a window showing the different weights of line in the architecture of the buildings and the various angles that they make.

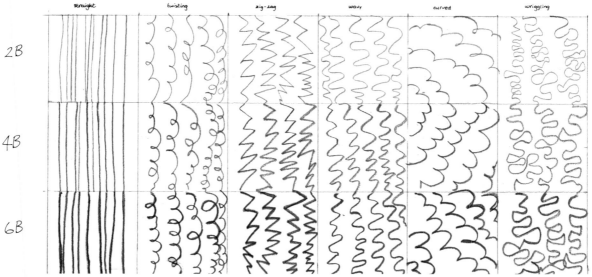

Lines in pencil – the finished exercise.

Lines in pencil

Always sharpen your pencils with a sharp craft knife or scalpel (X-acto knife). This gives you a much stronger point and is less wasteful of the pencil than using a pencil sharpener.

Attach the sheet of paper to the drawing board horizontally, and mark out a box measuring 15 × 30cm (6 × 12in.). Divide the box into 50mm (2in.) squares. Write the number of each of the different grades of pencil you are using down the left-hand side, next to the first three squares. Below each vertical line of boxes, write a different word to describe a type of line: for example, straight, twisting, zig-zag, wavy, curved, wriggling.

Start in the top left-hand corner box and fill it with lines according to the type you have chosen, using a 2B pencil. When you reach the bottom edge of that box, change to a 4B pencil and continue down, connecting the lines. Change to a 6B pencil for the bottom box. As you use the various grades of pencil, try different pressures on the point to see the different density of line. The greater the pressure, the darker the line will be.

Lines in dip pen and brush

On an A3 sheet of paper, attached vertically to the drawing board, mark out a box measuring 30 × 15cm (12 × 6in.) with a pencil and ruler. Mark out two lines at 50mm (2in.) intervals, running from top to bottom. Measure 50mm (2in.) down from the top of the box and mark out two lines 12mm (½in.) apart running horizontally across the paper. Measure another 50mm (2in.) from the lower line, and then draw another two horizontal lines 12mm (½in.) apart. Proceed in this way down the paper until you reach the bottom of the box.

In each of the 12mm (½in.) wide spaces beneath the boxes, write a word describing the type of line that you are trying to create. Write underneath the box for the bottom three squares. Then draw these lines in the boxes with Indian (India) ink, using both different nib widths and

brushes. You should try to make each line or group of lines within each box contrast with the next one. One way of achieving this contrast is to experiment with different nibs and brushes.

When you are making lines inside the boxes, try not to use a ruler; it is better to work freehand. Be patient about your ability to manoeuvre the pen or brush and don't worry about smudges.

Lines in dip pen and brush – the finished exercise.

Working from observation

By practising drawing different lines in pencil, dip pen and brush, you will begin to have an understanding of materials and their effects. Next is to learn how to look. The first exercise to develop the skill of co-ordinating your eye and your hand is to make a series of small line drawings in pencil and dip pen from observation. At this stage the question of proportion need not worry you. Just respond to what you see in front of you, the shape and movement of the line. These are your first tentative steps in observational drawing, so the results might seem rather limited but don't be discouraged.

Looking at straight lines

New students often complain of not being able to draw a straight line. Indeed, drawing straight lines freehand does take practice, but the following exercise will help. It will also start you looking properly at angles.

Attach an A3 sheet of paper horizontally to the drawing board. Draw a line down the middle of the paper in pencil. Work on either side of this line, alternating your drawings in dip pen with your drawings in pencil. If your pen seems to be clogging up with ink and not making a steady line, clean it in water.

Look at the top right-hand corner of the drawing board; you are now going to draw that angle. Make a dot on the paper (on the right-hand side) to represent the point where the two edges of the board meet. Look along the top line of your board and place another dot on the paper, about 75mm (3in.) to the left of the first. Now look down the right-hand side of the board and place a dot on the paper, about 75mm (3in.) below the original dot. Join the three dots, and you should have an angle of approximately 90 degrees.

This method of line construction gives points of reference as you plot angles and create straight lines. It is a good basis for building up an image on paper from observation.

Look around you in the room and draw different angles, either using the dot-line method to plot angles or just trying to draw straight lines from observation. It is difficult to draw a straight line longer than 15cm (6in.). If, however, you first make a series of dots at 75mm (3in.) intervals, it becomes easier. Fill the two halves of the A3 sheet with studies of angles and straight lines.

When you are working from observation, you should always glance from the subject to the drawing repeatedly and quickly.

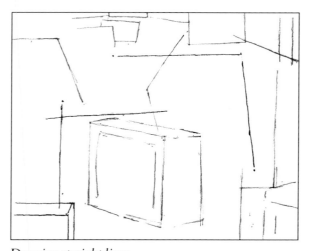

Drawing straight lines.

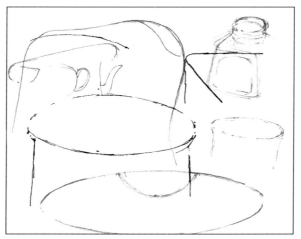

Drawing curves.

Looking at curves

Attach an A3 sheet of paper horizontally to the drawing board. Arrange an assortment of cups, saucepans, and other items that have simple curves, in front of you.

Using a dip pen and pencil alternately, create a series of curves based on those in the objects in front of you. As in the previous exercise, remember to keep glancing at the object and back to the paper. Try to draw each curve in an unbroken line without removing your pen or pencil from the paper, varying the shapes and sizes of the curves according to the objects in front of you. At first your curves may not flow smoothly, but you should soon be able to draw a curve with a single stroke of the pen or pencil.

After a number of attempts, when you feel more satisfied with your efforts, look around you in the room for any other curves such as the side of a fruit bowl or a lamp base and stand.

In the case of a more complex or larger curve, try drawing it by the dot-line method that you used to draw straight lines. Mark three dots, the middle one at the highest point of the curve and the others at either end. Join them together, again glancing at the object and back to the paper to help you get the right shape.

Looking at crumpled paper

The edge of a piece of crumpled paper has a combination of different lines. In some places it is straight; in others it can be crinkly. Drawing the outline of the paper, with these different lines is a good test of the skills you have started to develop.

Divide an A3 sheet of paper with a pencil line down the middle and attach it horizontally to the board. Then crumple an A4 piece of paper, so you have a shape that has a series of different contours. Place it on the table in front of you, preferably on a darker background.

Attempt to follow the line of the contours of the crumpled paper by observation and convey this on one half of the A3 paper in pencil or ink. You should try to make the density of line delicate, by varying the pressure on the point of the pencil or pen.

Change the shape or position of the crumpled piece of paper to get a different edge for each drawing on the two halves of the paper.

Drawing crumpled paper is a demanding exercise, so you will need to persevere. You could also try drawing other crumpled objects like cushions or a pile of washing. The line of your non-drawing hand is another interesting subject as it can take so many different positions.

A drawing of crumpled paper and the author's non-drawing hand.

Measurement and proportion

Perspective is a means of representing three-dimensional forms on a two-dimensional surface. The theory is the most difficult prospect for people starting to draw from observation, but it is essential to grasp in order to do representational drawings. The basic rules were developed during the early Italian Renaissance, and are still used today.

Right: Interior of the Kew Bridge Steam Museum. Using sight-size measurement as a framework, I worked in Indian (India) ink to create a tonal perspective of the architecture and machinery.

Measurement techniques

The practical process of sight-size measurement is the simplest way to teach yourself how to understand perspective. Sight-size means that the object should be the same size as it would appear to be if the paper were transparent and you simply traced the object on it at arm's length.

Look around your room and try this little experiment. Place a bottle 2 metres (6ft) away from you, at eye level; hold a pencil at arm's length and measure the bottle's height against the length of the pencil with one eye closed. Now place the bottle 4 metres (12ft) away and measure it again in the same way. The bottle should be considerably smaller against the length of the pencil.

The main principle of perspective is that the further away objects are, the smaller they appear to the eye. This is immediately discernible by sight-size measurement.

Before you start to measure an object, you should consider the following important points:

Position Keep the same position in relationship to the object. While measuring, hold your head at the angle you wish to draw at.

Eyes Look at an object in front of you with your left eye closed, then open your left eye and close your right. Repeat this procedure a few times in quick succession. The object jumps from side to side.

Arm When you measure, keep your arm fully extended and straight.

Pencil Keep your pencil vertical while measuring. Imagine that there is a pane of glass at arm's length and hold your pencil against it.

Accuracy Try to be correct, but bear in mind that total precision is not possible. The sight-size system will help give your observational drawing a simple structural base, but is not meant to produce mathematical accuracy.

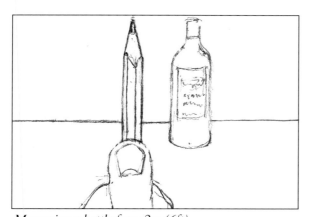

Measuring a bottle from 2m (6ft).

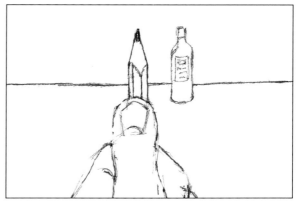

Measuring the same bottle from 4m (12ft).

Drawing an object sight-size

Place a cup 15cm (6in.) beyond arm's length on a table. Measure the cup's height with your arm extended, one eye closed and your pencil vertical.

Mark the top point of the rim of the cup on the paper; do the same with the bottom point of the cup to the distance indicated by your pencil.

Next, measure the distance from the mark you have made for the top of the rim to the lowest point of the rim, and mark it. You should now have three marks directly in line with one another. Draw a straight line through these marks.

To work out the width of the cup, measure horizontally across it from rim to rim. Place two marks to represent these points on the drawing. Draw a straight line extending horizontally through these marks.

Join the marks with curves to create the rim of the cup. When drawing curves, remember to move your eyes from drawing to object quickly – look and draw. The rim is now complete.

To draw the sides of the cup, measure them by sight, make two marks and connect. Draw the bottom of the cup in the same way.

Next draw the handle of the cup by measuring the top, bottom and side points of the handle, make three marks and then connect them, using the scanning process described above.

Look at the inside of the handle and draw its shape in relationship to the outside edge.

Finally, draw the table edge behind the cup, measuring the distance from the top of the rim.

Now repeat the drawing, this time placing it 45cm (18in.) beyond arm's length. Compare the size of the cup in your first and second drawings. This will demonstrate clearly how objects appear smaller as they move further away from you.

When connecting your marks, try to use them only as general reference. You should look from the object to your drawing, scanning the images swiftly rather than pondering. In this way, comparisons of the marks and actuality can be made more efficiently.

Joining the first three marks that indicate the rim.

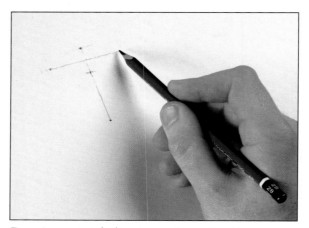

Drawing a straight line across the cup's width.

Drawing the rim of the cup with curves.

The sides and bottom edge of the cup drawn in.

Putting in the cup handle, after measuring it.

After measuring the distance from the top point of the rim to the table edge, the line of the table edge is drawn.

Drawing a group of objects

When you draw a combination of objects, the spaces between them are just as important as the outline of each item and its proportions. You should treat each object as part of the group. In this way you are better able to involve the relationship between each item, which is very important in terms of creating a cohesive scale drawing. In the early stages of such a drawing, you should try to get used to leaving the objects in an unfinished form.

In this exercise you should measure both the objects and the spaces between them to sight-size.

Place a group of four objects on a table in front of you. The objects should include a cylinder (for example, a tall glass, an aerosol can, or a tube container of talcum powder), a sphere (a tennis ball, a softball, or an orange), an angular or curved shape (a pepper mill, a large perfume bottle, or a sauce bottle), and an irregular sphere (a large potato, stones or large pebbles). The objects should not be higher than 20cm (8in.) and not

smaller than 75mm (3in.) Arrange them as shown, with the cylinder in the centre.

Make a mark with a 2B pencil for the top left-hand point of the cylinder in the top centre of the paper (point A). Measure the distance using sight-size to the irregular sphere below. Make a mark (point B), then draw a line between the two marks. From point B, measure across to the far right-hand side of the regular sphere, make a mark and draw part of its curve. This is point C.

Now, work out the horizontal dimension, from point B to the far left-hand side of the angular shape. This is point D, mark and draw part of its edge. If the table edge crosses the AB line, measure from point A and draw it in.

Again, measure horizontally from point B across to the other side of the cylinder. As this is obscured by the sphere, you will have to judge its position and make a mark. Draw the line of the cylinder. Measure diagonally downwards from point C to the far left-hand edge of the irregular sphere. Mark this point E and draw part of its edge on your drawing.

The objects arranged on a table.

The first lines emerging.

Drawing in the line for the table edge as it crosses the AB line.

Measure diagonally upwards from point E to the top left–hand point of the angular shape (point F). Mark and draw part of its edge. From point F, measure to the highest point of the cylinder and draw its top curve.

Now that you have drawn the basic framework of the objects, start to measure and look at them individually. Draw their outlines. Measure the distances between shapes that are next to each other and mark them. Keep the drawing simple, concentrating on the outlines of the objects.

Finally, draw the contour lines on the objects. At this stage, stick to lines and do not worry

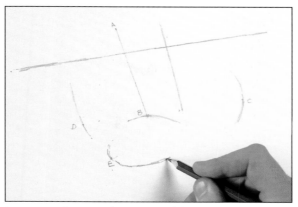

Putting in the irregular curves of the potato.

Drawing the top curve of the cylinder.

Giving the objects their simple outlines.

about tone. Make marks, shapes and lines that suggest the objects' form. Use an eraser to clarify your drawing where necessary, and to remove the lines that run through the objects.

If you have to leave the drawing unfinished for a few days, mark the positions of the objects on the table with masking tape (alternatively, you could place a sheet of paper under the objects when setting the group up, and draw round them to mark their position on this). Try to leave your chair in the same position, or make a note of exactly where you placed it, so that when you come back you will be in the same position in relation to the objects.

Finally, making marks, shapes and lines that suggest the objects' forms.

Further ideas

Enlarging and reducing

The process of sight-size measurement creates a framework and guidelines for you to work within. If you want to make a drawing that is larger than sight-size, start by measuring the objects sight-size, but then double the measurements. The same process can be used to reduce the image: measure the objects to sight-size, but then halve the measurements. These techniques of enlarging and reducing a scene are useful when you need to work on a small scale or want to cover a larger area.

Format

A simple method of extending your understanding of measurement and proportion is to change the format and size of your paper. Cut an A3 (18 × 12in.) sheet of cartridge (drawing) paper into different-sized squares, rectangles and circles. Make drawings in outline that cover the whole of each piece of paper. On a thin, horizontal rectangular shape, for instance, you could draw a slice or section only of a scene, such as the shopping arcade (mall) I drew. On the round piece I chose a flower to echo the format. You could also use different measurements: sight-size, half sight-size or twice sight-size.

As an exercise in understanding format and measurement I drew a series of different subjects on different shaped pieces of paper. The study of a figure in a landscape was done sight-size; the scene of the shops and the doorway drawings were made to half sight-size; the flower and the figure were twice sight-size.

Tonal techniques

Line is a very beautiful medium to work in on its own, but its representational range can be enhanced by combination with tone. Tone is the world of colour represented in black and white. To show mass, tonal areas have to be drawn, and the graduations of light and dark need to be realized.

Before you start to work on a tonal drawing, make this simple comparison. Switch on your television set, and if it is colour turn down the brightness and turn up the contrast. You should see a limited image that seems to be essentially only light and dark. As you look at the image, increase the brightness. The greys should start to appear, creating more definition and more intricate forms.

Now go and sit a few paces away from a window. Slowly close your eyes until you are squinting. You should see a limited image with great contrast, like the television screen without the brightness. As you slowly open your eyes, the forms will become more defined, and the variety of tones between light and dark will become greater. The eye can pick out many more tones than the television image.

As with the television, the materials used when drawing cannot define the range of tones that the eye perceives. The subtlety has to be simplified.

You will need
- ☐ a drawing board
- ☐ A3 (18 × 12in.) cartridge (drawing) paper
- ☐ 2B, 4B and 6B pencils
- ☐ a dip pen and nibs
- ☐ Indian (India) ink
- ☐ brushes
- ☐ charcoal sticks
- ☐ a plastic eraser
- ☐ a ruler
- ☐ masking tape
- ☐ a sharp craft knife
- ☐ a paper stump (stomp)
- ☐ a stacking palette (cabinet nest)
- ☐ a container of water

The tonal range picked out by the human eye.

Definition is reduced when squinting.

Dark to light and light to dark

As in line, the first step is to get accustomed to perceiving and representing linear shapes, so with tone, the first step is to become familiar with basic tonal techniques.

Attach an A3 sheet of paper to the board vertically. Mark a pencil line horizontally across the centre of the paper.

Mark 22 straight lines at 12mm (½in.) intervals, 25mm (1in.) above the central line. Write the letter D (for 'dark') underneath the first vertical channel. Mark the next channels, from left to right, 1 to 9. Mark the tenth channel L (for 'light'), the next channels 9 to 1 and the last D.

Using a pencil create a deep tone with heavy, merged marks in the first channel. Go on to the next channel, making the marks slightly less black. Continue until the middle channel which should be left clear. Then continue, making each channel to the right gradually darker again. The art is to judge it so as to achieve an evenness to the increasing lightness and darkness.

Using a pencil alone is very unlikely to produce accurate results. Work into the graduated channels with an eraser, lightening areas, or use a paper stump (stomp) to spread the carbon and create subtle tones. You can also use your fingers.

You may have to work up and down the series of channels, lightening or darkening as you go; this is quite acceptable, do not expect to get it right the first time.

Pencil
Pencil can be used to produce shading, and often is in a sketchbook. However, when you begin to look at tone, pencil gets you involved with drawing only small areas and detail, whereas one should first master overall tonal scale. Charcoal and ink are much better for this. When using pencil for tone you can use the edge of the lead as well as the point.

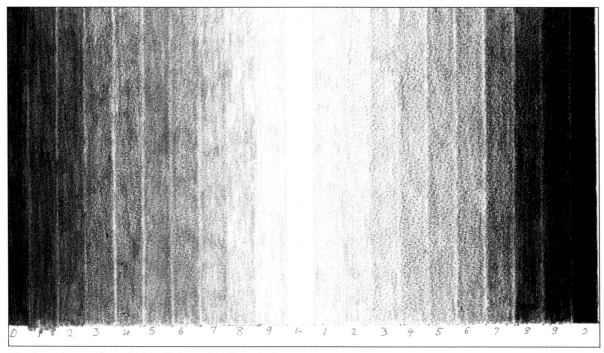

Graduated tones from dark to light and light to dark.

39

Using charcoal

Underneath your first tonal exercise in pencil, mark eleven 25mm (1in.) vertical straight lines, about 160 mm (6½ in.) high. Mark a straight diagonal line from the top left–hand corner to the bottom right–hand corner.

At the top left–hand corner above your first channel write the letter L, then write from 1 to 8 above the next eight channels and the letter D above the last channel. Write in the same letter and numerals, but in reverse order, at the bottom of the channels. The letter D denotes the darkest tone, the letter L the lightest tone.

This time build a series of tones in the top section above the diagonal line, working from light to dark in gradual steps with a stick of charcoal. In the section below the diagonal line, work from dark to light in gradual steps.

Although charcoal can be messy and difficult to preserve due to its powdery quality, its subtlety in tonal gradations is such that it is well worth persevering to learn how to use it. You may well need to use a paper stump or your fingers to spread the charcoal. A plastic eraser is useful to take away built-up tones of charcoal.

Using a paper stump to spread charcoal.

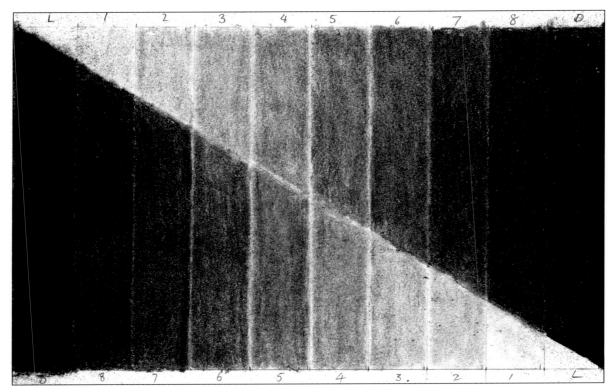

Tonal steps – the finished exercise.

Working with ink

Tone can be achieved with different intensities of ink. Pencil out a 25cm (10in.) square on an A3 sheet of paper. Draw a diagonal line from the top left-hand corner to the bottom right-hand corner, then draw another line from the top right-hand corner to the bottom left.

Mark six points at 25mm (1in.) intervals on each diagonal line starting from the central point. Connect the points with straight lines, creating a series of squares. You should be left with a border of 6mm (¼in.) on the outside.

Mark the central square D, denoting darkest. Number the outside squares from 1 to 5. Leave the remaining border completely clear.

Now take a plastic palette. To obtain the gradation of tones you need, put pure ink in one section. Put pure ink in the next section, but add a small quantity of water, progressively adding more water to each section until you have a series of different washes that become lighter.

Working flat on the table to prevent the ink running, use a brush to make the central square of your tonal square completely black with pure ink. As you work towards the outside of the subsequent squares, make each one slightly lighter by using a more diluted wash.

Use a flat-ended brush to make the washes. Work as swiftly as you can but try to keep the tones created by the brush even and straight. After each different square is completed, wash your brush in clean water and remove the excess water from the bristles with a tissue.

It takes time to learn how to make even washes. Initially, the effect of gradation from the black square in the centre to the white of the border is more important than an exact, smooth wash.

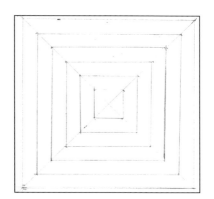

Above left: The tonal square drawn out; with some washes (below left); and completed (right).

Cutting the square notches in the top section.

Cutting the slits in the back section.

Making notches in one of the side sections.

Tonal theatre

A good way of learning to see how objects are made up of light and dark tone areas, is to use a tonal theatre or light modulator. The tonal theatre or light modulator is quite easy and quick to make and will help your appreciation of tone by confining your vision.

Making the tonal theatre

When cutting out card, always use a drawing board to protect the surface of the table. It is also helpful to have an extra strip of card under the area you are going to cut; this stops the knife embedding itself in the drawing board and prevents the surface from getting too many gouges. Always use a craft knife and a sturdy ruler to keep the cuts straight. Make sure the blade is sharp, but keep your fingers at a safe distance.

Place the card on the drawing board on a firm surface. Mark and cut out two rectangles measuring 32.5 × 25cm (13 × 10in.) and two rectangles measuring 27.5 × 25cm (11 × 10in.).

Place one of the larger rectangles on the drawing board. This will be the top section. Mark a 25mm (1in.) square in pencil in each corner. Cut these squares out with a craft knife.

Place the other larger rectangle on the drawing board vertically. This will be the back section. Draw lines horizontally right across the card with the ruler 25mm (1in.) in from both ends. Measure 40mm (1½in.) in at each of the four ends of the two horizontal lines and mark these points. The middle section of these lines should measure 17.5cm (7in.). Cut slits horizontally between these points with a craft knife as shown.

The sides of the tonal theatre are identical. Place one of the smaller rectangles on the board so that the 27.5cm (11in.) edges are at the top and bottom. On the right-hand side of the rectangle, mark and cut out two corner pieces 50mm (2in.) deep and 25mm (1in.) wide. Measure 50mm (2in.) down from the top of the card. Mark a line horizontally across the board. Measure 18mm

(¾in.) in to the left of the top corner point and to the right of the left-hand end, and cut slits along the horizontal line with a craft knife for the back section to slot into. Repeat the process with the other smaller rectangle to make the second side.

Assemble the tonal theatre by pushing the sides through the back slits. Then push the top through the side slits. Widen the slits if they are too tight to take the card.

Using the tonal theatre

When you have assembled your card theatre, place it on a table and put different objects inside. These should vary in their surface, shape and material. Try to imagine them as small sculptures. Look out for interesting things you could use: small artifacts, little boxes or anything that you may have collected on country walks or when beachcombing. You should choose a contrasting selection of objects; you can also try various combinations of articles in different positions. You could even make some objects yourself, or wrap some of the items in paper or material to disguise or soften the shapes.

Move the theatre around on the table so that you can see the variety of light and the way it falls inside the theatre.

You will find that by putting objects in this box you cut out distractions and can concentrate on their tonal features. Draw them in ink or charcoal.

Further ideas

When you have become familiar with the tonal theatre, you can experiment with different effects. To get different lighting on the objects inside it, cut shapes or slots in the top. Experiment with dramatic lighting effects at night by placing an angled desk lamp or a bedside lamp above the box. Make studies of different objects in charcoal; try to achieve a strong contrast of tone to match what you see. Also draw something in pencil, concentrating on just a section of the theatre rather than showing the whole thing.

Try also putting a mirror in the tonal theatre, either a piece of mirror specially cut to fit in, or a hand mirror. Place this mirror under a single object and do a drawing of it looking at the shape of both the object itself and its mirror image.

You can also create several small studies across one sheet of cartridge paper, changing the object every time you finish a drawing. Work on each drawing for no more than 15 minutes. You can achieve different effects by moving your theatre around to change the direction of the light.

Slotting the side piece into the back section.

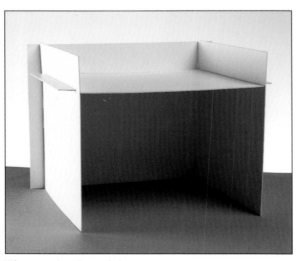

The completed tonal theatre.

Projects: Tonal drawings

This drawing will take you step-by-step through the process of working in charcoal from dark to light. Charcoal is often worked this way; it involves first covering the paper with a layer of charcoal, and then removing it in parts. The commentary is merely a guideline for you to follow, not the definitive method. Try to develop your own techniques for looking and working from my approach. As charcoal is difficult to manipulate on a small scale, it is often advisable to work larger than sight-size, as in this project.

A charcoal drawing

You will need
■ a drawing board
■ A2 (24 × 18in.) paper
■ grey paper or card
■ stick charcoal
■ a charcoal pencil
■ compressed charcoal
■ a dip pen and nibs
■ Indian (India) ink
■ brushes
■ a paper stump (stomp)
■ a plastic eraser
■ masking tape
■ spray fixative
■ a ruler
■ a soft rag
■ a container of water

Above: I selected three objects for my arrangement that had a combination of contrasting lines.
Left: The finished drawing.

Setting up the tonal theatre

The tonal theatre was set in front of me on a table. Underneath it I placed a piece of grey paper, allowing a distance of about 60cm (2ft) from the edge of my drawing board (when sitting in my drawing position) to where I placed the theatre. I then selected three objects from my collection of articles that I found interesting, and arranged them so that I would use the back, middle and front sections of the theatre.

Basic outline

After attaching to my drawing board a single A2 sheet of cartridge (drawing) paper cut down to fit the board, I positioned myself directly in front of the theatre. The first job was to make a basic outline drawing using charcoal pencil of the frame of the theatre to twice sight-size. It was important to be as accurate as possible (within reason, of course) with the measurements, as this was the structure from which the tonal arrangement would emerge. The twice sight-size scale meant that I had to use a ruler as well as my pencil, to take the measurements with. I made a couple of small charcoal marks on the outside edges of my theatre drawing to indicate the main lines. These would be obliterated by the thick charcoal layer I was about to apply.

Establishing the lightest point
In order to get a clear idea of the strongest tones I looked at the objects inside the theatre with my eyes half closed, as if squinting in sunlight. The very lightest section, which was the crescendo of light in the theatre, was to be left completely free of charcoal in my drawing. Within the rest of the framework I applied a thick layer of stick charcoal, which I worked into the paper with bold strokes, creating a deep tonal layer of charcoal covering almost the entire frame of the theatre.

Creating mid-tone
I looked at the tonal theatre again with my eyes half closed. The back wall of the theatre seemed to be a mid-tone; certainly it was lighter than the floor of the theatre. Using a soft rag, I very lightly erased a layer of charcoal from the back wall of the theatre to create a mid-tone layer.

Starting on the objects
Taking a piece of compressed charcoal, which is darker than stick charcoal, I started to measure with a ruler and pencil and draw the outline of the objects inside the theatre to twice sight-size. I could quite easily see the shapes emerging from the stick charcoal layer. It is important that the measurements of the objects relate to each other and the frame of the theatre.

Light sections
With the lightest section of my drawing free from charcoal, I wanted to bring out the other light areas inside the tonal theatre. Again, I squinted, looking at the theatre to check the relative tonal values. Using a soft rag, I lightly erased a section

Drawing out the basic outline of the tonal theatre.

Covering almost the whole surface in charcoal.

Creating the mid-tones.

of the foreground of the theatre to indicate the light entering it. With an eraser I highlighted those parts of the roll of tape caught by the light (the sharp edge of a plastic eraser allows you to be more controlled and remove more charcoal).

Dark sections
I then had to put in the darkest lines and sections. The darkest areas seemed to be at the back edges of the theatre, around and in between the objects. I again used compressed charcoal to draw in these darkest sections. At this point in the drawing I knew the lightest and darkest parts of the drawing and had drawn them in. All the other tones had to be between these values.

Increasing definition
I stepped back and looked at the drawing from a distance. The drawing needed more mid-tones, so I worked these using a plastic eraser, a soft rag and sometimes my fingers. I also used the compressed charcoal to emphasize some lines and shadows. I

assessed the tone by frequently glancing at the subject, then working on my drawing. The definition of the shadows around the objects became more obvious by the removal of a layer of charcoal from the objects themselves, and by application of the compressed charcoal. The process of removal of charcoal and adding to and slightly changing the lines using the charcoal pencil to create more exacting shapes was completed at this stage.

Finishing off
In this last step I used the plastic eraser to create sharp, light lines at the front corner of the theatre. Then with the stump (stomp) I merged and spread the mid-tones in the foreground and midground. I then decided that the drawing was finished, so I used a spray fixative (always follow the instructions carefully) to protect the drawing and prevent it smudging. You can use a soft rag gently to remove thin lines of charcoal if necessary before spraying a drawing with fixative.

Drawing the outline of the shapes against the charcoal background.

Removing a charcoal layer with an eraser.

Using compressed charcoal for the darkest sections.

Merging the mid-tones with a paper stump.

A drawing in pen and wash

Having worked from dark to light in the last drawing, this one uses mid-tones with washes and lines, working more from light to dark. Although one can work from light to dark with charcoal, it is the only way of working with ink washes as the ink, once applied, cannot be removed like unfixed charcoal. The method one uses will depend a little on the darkness desired for the end result, but is mainly determined by taste. Only towards the end of the drawing is the darkest tone established. The process of slowly creating a series of transparent tonal washes is an excellent starting point for anyone who wishes to paint in watercolour.

Do not forget the principles you have learned in measurement and proportion drawings; try to use them in conjunction with these new methods.

Arranging the composition

I set up the tonal theatre in the same position as for the charcoal drawing. The objects were arranged so that they overlapped but still filled the entire space of the theatre.

I then positioned myself directly in front of the theatre, resting the drawing board with stretched paper on my lap and against the edge of the table. I made a sight-size outline drawing of the frame of the theatre in soft charcoal pencil.

The arrangement of objects inside the tonal theatre.

The finished drawing in pen and wash.

Drawing the basic outlines of the objects.

Basic outline

Using charcoal pencil, I started to measure and draw the outline of the objects within the theatre. As I drew, I observed carefully the shapes between the objects as well as the objects themselves. I kept the lines faint as in the first step.

Drawing the mid-tones

Judging that this would be the number needed, I mixed four different washes in my stacking palette. They represented an even progression across the tonal scale; the last wash had just a touch of water added. It is important to test the strength of each wash in a corner of the stretched paper before applying it to the drawing. You can then lighten or darken the wash if it does not seem right. This testing is especially important in the later stages of a drawing when the scope for correction is less.

I looked at the darker and medium areas of the theatre and the objects using the technique of screwing up my eyes to determine their exact location. Then with a flat-ended brush I drew them all in a mid-tone wash. As I applied the washes, I kept looking at the subtle changes in the shapes of the objects in relation to the theatre, changing them as I wished. This was not just a matter of filling in the drawn-out spaces, but was crucial to the whole drawing. I then went over the darkest areas in a slightly darker wash.

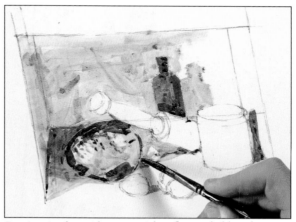

Putting in the mid-tones with a flat-ended brush.

The shapes emerge

Using a slightly lighter wash, I applied another layer of tone to the areas in the tonal theatre that appeared to use the next lightest once I had established a range of mid-tones in the drawing. I then felt ready to tackle the darker edges of the theatre and the objects, and drew them in with a dip pen. At this point in the drawing I was looking at the general shapes, and not getting involved with the patterns on the objects or with any detail.

Achieving contrast

Some of the areas I had drawn in with mid-tone washes now seemed too light in contrast with the darker areas I had just drawn in, so I went over these in darker washes.

Drawing the darker edges in dip pen.

The darkest tones

In this final step, I washed in the darkest tones using my round-ended brushes. The washes very often overlapped and started to provide detail. The shadows became more defined; the feeling was that of looking at an entrance to an enclosure which was the effect I had been hoping to create. The final washes were added to create a strong contrast and I was now satisfied with the drawing.

Creating a contrast with the final, darkest washes.

Mixed media techniques

Drawing in mixed media might sound like a contemporary invention, but the process has in fact been around for centuries. Mixed media means using combinations of different materials together, such as pencil and ink. Exciting patterns and textures can be created as you experiment with different combinations of materials. These exercises will help you to explore the richness and variety of marks, lines and tone. You should try to make each one have an individual quality; you aren't just doodling, you are exploring a vocabulary for future drawings.

Guidelines are given in each of the different exercises as to how to create the marks, but they are only suggestions and you should follow them loosely. It is important to create your own qualities and to be prepared to combine the unexpected and the accidental in these exercises.

Degas 'Ballet Dancers' (detail) 473 × 625mm (19 × 25in.). A quick study in line on toned paper captures the dancers' momentary movement.

You will need
- ☐ a drawing board
- ☐ A3 (18 × 12in.) paper
- ☐ 2B, 4B and 6B pencils
- ☐ a dip pen, nibs and ink
- ☐ a bamboo pen
- ☐ brushes
- ☐ white oil crayon
- ☐ white gouache
- ☐ charcoal
- ☐ a charcoal pencil
- ☐ a plastic eraser
- ☐ a ruler
- ☐ a sharp craft knife
- ☐ a stacking palette (cabinet nest)
- ☐ rubber-based glue
- ☐ a container of water

Mixed media line techniques

On an A3 sheet of paper mark out a rectangle measuring 37.5 × 15cm (15 × 6in.) with a pencil and ruler. Divide the rectangle into five rectangles measuring 15 × 7.5cm (6 × 3in.). Mark these boxes 1 to 5 from left to right.

1 Draw a series of lines the length of the box alternating between pen and brush. Make the lines of different widths and draw them in one movement; do not worry about how straight they are. Using your waxed crayon, zig-zag a line across the width of the box, dragging the still-wet ink as you go.

2 Starting at the top of the box make a looped line in 4B pencil that runs to the bottom. Using charcoal pencil, start to create a spiral effect by overlapping the pencil lines as you loop to the bottom of the page. Do the same with stick charcoal and brush and ink.

3 Draw an oval in charcoal pencil that is approximately the length of the box. Draw a continuous pencil line in a random manner looping and zig-zagging through the oval. With the dip pen, draw a series of tight, thin lines in your pencil loops. Using a brush, splatter or flick ink on to the central part of the oval, first covering the other boxes with spare paper to prevent their getting spotted with ink. Finally make a few random spotted marks with your brush and bamboo pen to add contrast to the line.

4 Gently draw a series of thick lines in stick charcoal across the box. You should vary the width of line, leaving some gaps of plain white paper. Draw a series of random charcoal pencil lines with a finely sharpened charcoal pencil over the stick charcoal. Vary the width of the charcoal pencil line by changing the pressure on the point as you move across the box. Using the sharp edge of a plastic eraser, rub out a series of sharp lines across the surface of the box.

5 Using charcoal pencil, draw sharp lines all across the box with different tonal gradations. Smudge these lines together in places with your fingers. When you feel that you have a sufficient tonal range, draw over the top in dip pen. Try to make as many varied lines in dip pen as you can.

Write under each box the combination of materials you have used. This will help you later if you wish to research more line or tone mixed media techniques and experiment further with the effects you can create.

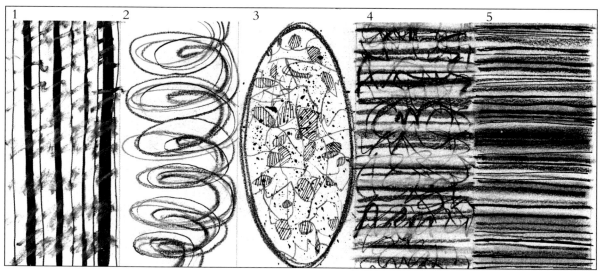

The finished exercise.

Mixed media tonal techniques

The materials for this exercise are the same as those used for the techniques in line except that a jar of water is also needed. Draw out the boxes using the same measurements as in the line techniques exercise.

With the tonal techniques a certain amount of physical pressure is needed, both in erasing vigorously and in scratching the surface of the drawing to create the slightly raised textures that appear as subtle patterns.

1 Pour a tiny amount of ink into a stacking palette, press your fingers into the ink and apply the resulting finger-prints at different strengths across the whole of the box. Then place a small object with a textured or raised surface, such as a metal food grater or a coin, under your dry finger-prints and make a series of small rubbings. Contrast the patterns created by the finger-prints with the rubbings.

2 Draw a variety of diagonal lines in oil crayon from the bottom left-hand corner to the top right-hand corner of the box. Mix Indian (India) ink with an equal quantity of water in your palette. Apply this mid-tone wash across the whole of the box. You will see that the wax of the crayon resists the water, and that the white lines will appear against the grey of the background.

3 Starting with a stick of charcoal, and then going on to a charcoal pencil, compressed charcoal, and finally a 4B pencil, make a series of horizontal lines across the box to create a tonal sandwich. Apply each material in turn across the entire width of the box, making the width of each line the same as your drawing instrument. Leave occasional glimpses of paper beneath your lines to add contrast.

4 Make a thin layer of charcoal across the box. With a 6B pencil and a charcoal pencil draw looping pencil lines and zig-zagging charcoal lines over your charcoal layer. In oil crayon, draw a series of dense lines together at random parts of the box. On top of this mixture of line and tone, make a series of small tonal ovals in charcoal pencil and pencil.

Using a ruler make a series of sharp vertical lines 6 mm (¼in.) apart across your box. Erase every other line as much as you can, to create a contrast of tone and line.

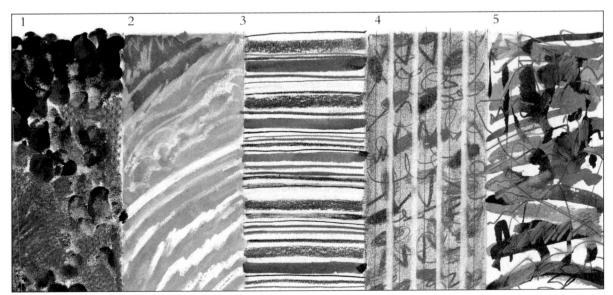

The finished exercise.

5 Draw a series of large ink lines in brush across your box. Then draw over the top of these lines in pencil even if they are still wet; be sure to press hard with your pencil. Draw another series of large ink lines across your box. Using oil crayon, try to bring out the line of the pencil against the ink, varying the pressure of the oil crayon as you rub. Finally rub out different sections of your box with an eraser to create subtle changes of pattern and texture.

Henry Moore 'Shelter Scene – Bunks and Sleepers' (detail) 480 × 426mm (19 × 17in.). Henry Moore uses a combination of varied media to create character and a sense of environment through tone.

Further ideas

To try out these techniques, you should choose different still-life subjects to draw. A section or detail of a leafy plant, a bowl of fruit, or a vase of flowers would be ideal.

Gouache resist

Divide an A3 sheet of paper into four rectangles and cut these out using a ruler and a knife. Mark out a 10cm (4in.) square in pencil in the centre of one of the rectangular sheets.

Using the white gouache, start to paint, working from the still-life subject that you have chosen. Try to vary the thickness of the lines and marks, and concentrate on the patterns within the objects and their linear quality.

When the gouache has dried completely, paint an even coat of undiluted Indian ink over the whole square. Allow that to dry.

Place the paper under a running tap, and let the gouache wash away, taking out the ink in those areas too. Rub gently with your fingers or use a soft brush until the whole image you have painted has reappeared. Place the wet paper on your drawing board to dry. You can at this stage stretch the paper (see pages 24–5) to ensure that it stays flat when it is completely dry.

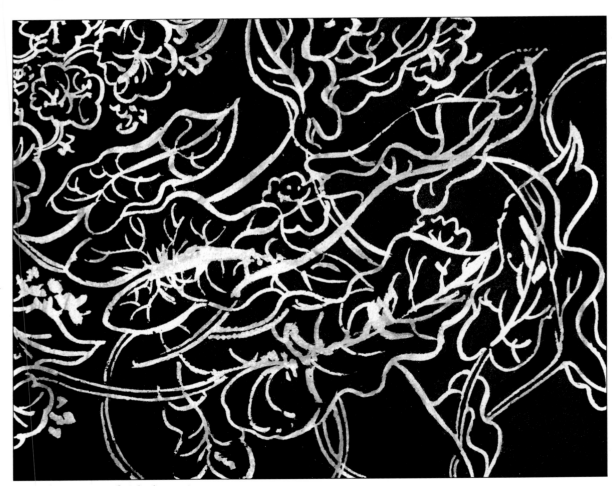

Gouache resist – a finished exercise.

Scratch technique – a finished exercise.

Glue resist – a finished exercise.

Scratch technique

Mark out a 10cm (4in.) square in the centre of one of the prepared rectangles as described above in the gouache resist technique. To prevent the paper from buckling, you may wish to stretch the paper now (see pages 24–5). If so, allow the paper to dry before continuing with the exercise.

Paint a dense, even coat of undiluted ink over the whole square. Allow the ink to dry thoroughly.

Cover the whole square again, this time with a thick layer of white oil crayon. Go over the square several times so that it becomes completely white, and you cannot see the ink underneath. Make sure that you build up a thick layer of oil crayon as this will ensure you get very dark lines when you scratch into the surface.

Using a sharp craft knife, start to scratch away at the surface you have created. You will find that this will reveal the dark lines of the ink, in contrast to the white background. Using this scratching method, draw the image you have chosen and try to achieve the same qualities as in the gouache resist exercise, but using a very different technique.

Glue resist

Once again, mark out a 10cm (4in.) square in the centre of a prepared rectangle. Paint the image, this time with the glue, and allow it to dry thoroughly. Pots of glue are often supplied with a brush, but you may need a thin brush to vary the thickness of the marks. It need only be a cheap brush or an old one as the glue may ruin it for other use.

When the glue has hardened, paint the square completely with an even coat of Indian ink. Once the ink has dried, rub at the surface gently with your fingers and you will find that the glue will start to peel away from the paper, revealing a clean white image.

Project: A window in mixed media

In this project I decided to do two drawings of the same window from close to and from further away, using the mixed media techniques developed in the last section. Whereas each of these could have been executed in simple tone, the interplay of line, tone and light that one gets from a window lent itself better to the more complex medium.

The first drawing was a partial view of the window. By moving my chair back a couple of metres, but still positioning it in the same relationship to the window, I could then change the focus and include the window. Both drawings started with some simple measurements, made to sight-size, of the objects in the composition. When I was satisfied with these, I then drew them in quickly. This is often a good way to start a drawing, but you have to watch out for it becoming too loose when you are drawing quickly, and be ready to make more measurements in order to reassert the structure. Measurement is a useful tool, but I find that it must not be allowed to begin to dominate the spirit of an image.

You will need
- a drawing board
- A3 (18 × 12in.) cartridge (drawing) paper
- a 2B pencil
- a charcoal pencil
- stick charcoal
- a bamboo pen and ink
- brushes
- a white oil crayon
- a plastic eraser
- a paper stump (stomp)
- a stacking palette (cabinet nest)
- tissues
- a container of water

The finished drawing of the window (partial view).

Window – partial view

A partial view of the window set up.

Setting up

First, I stretched the sheet of cartridge paper on to my drawing board and set myself up close to the window. With the board balanced on my lap and my materials all within easy reach I focused on a small section of the window, the table, net curtains and plants.

Establishing the basic structure

Working in pencil, I made some basic sight–size measurements of the composition. To make the drawing manageable with the details clear and at the same time show most of the plant, I decided it needed to be sight–size.

I marked the section of the window frame in pencil and drew it in lightly, and then drew in the position of the plants in pencil and the lines of the net curtain in white oil crayon.

This initial stage has to be done very carefully, as a drawing whose basic structure is not properly established is difficult to get into proportion. While doing this drawing I glanced frequently from the drawing to the subject.

Filling in detail

In a light wash, and using a round-ended brush, I set about starting to fill in the shapes of the plants, window frames and net curtains. I did not

measure these lines but used the basic framework of my composition in pencil as a guide. The wash was made up as I went along, which gave me the opportunity to create some varieties in tone. I made very basic, thin washed lines to represent the net curtains.

Light tones

The lightest area in my composition was to the left of the plants where the light came in. I decided to leave this blank using the tone of the paper. The next lightest areas were the table top and net curtains where the light played on them. With an oil crayon I made bold lines and spotted marks on the areas that reflected this sensation, in the first stage of a resist technique.

Drawing the basic composition sight-size.

Laying a wash with a round-ended brush.

Using the oil crayon to create the resist surface.

Applying the wash over the oil crayon.

Applying a wash to the resist

Before applying a wash to the resist it was necessary to establish the contrasts in the composition, so I went over the darker leaves with a dark wash. When this was done I could then go over the table and curtains with a light wash, trying to make the wash reflect what I could see: light playing against the texture of the net curtain. The oil crayon repels the water of the wash, keeping these areas even lighter.

Supplying darker tones

I now felt ready to start on the darker tones. I went over the darkest areas of the side of the table and the earth in the pots with a dark wash. Using a charcoal pencil, I drew the outlines of the leaves and table edge in line, as they seemed to need emphasizing.

Final light touches

Finally, I scanned the whole of the small scene at arm's length to see what else needed doing. I decided that areas of the table top, curtains, stems and leaves were still too faint so I went over them again with a dark wash. I also felt that the curtains looked rather flat so I drew in gestural lines with the white oil crayon to give the sensation of the light shimmering against the darker shapes of the ferns.

Using a charcoal pencil to emphasize the edges.

Making gestural lines with oil crayon.

Window – full view

I moved back from my original position to give myself a good overall view of the window. This meant that I was now going to be working against the light. It was therefore even more important to establish the lightest and darkest tones in the drawing, so that the tonal proportions would be easier to attain as they fell between these extremes.

The drawing board was positioned in the same way as for the partial view drawing. When I had got this right I measured the window to sight-size as this scale seemed to fit the vertical format that I had chosen.

The framework

Using a 2B pencil for a soft line, I drew the frame of the window in lightly, making basic sight-size measurements to get the scale correct. Constantly glancing from the drawing to the subject I then scanned the plants and drew them in too. The lines of the plants are loose and flowing and had to be drawn so as not to appear rigid.

Applying darker tones

This time I elected to handle the darker areas first. The dark-toned sections of the window frame were drawn in thick charcoal, leaving the edges around it that catch the light free from charcoal.

A full view of the window set up.

The finished drawing.

Drawing the lines of the plants.

When I had finished making the tonal layer of charcoal I worked it into the paper using a paper stump (stomp) which let me achieve subtle gradations of the charcoal. I then used the plastic eraser to remove any unwanted charcoal. Next, the stump was ideal for making the lines for the plants in front of the window, providing a gentle spread of the layer of charcoal.

I created a light tonal layer of charcoal on the wall and drew in the shadow of the window frame by spreading the charcoal with the stump and erasing with the edge of a plastic eraser.

Establishing the darkest areas
At this point in the drawing I wanted to find the darkest areas. Squinting, I could see that the edges that catch the light on the window frame had the darkest lines next to them. Using brush and ink for the blackness I drew them in. The edges of the plant pot were the darkest section of the subject so I made these black using a bamboo pen.

Emphasizing light
Having done the dark areas, I then turned to the lighter ones. The net curtains were not to be shown in great detail so I drew them in a wash of ink mixed with a little water and applied with a round-ended brush. I then looked at the pots and plants and drew them in short lines using two washes, one darker than that used on the curtains.

Conveying light
Around the outside of the window the bright edges that caught the light needed sharpening, so I used a plastic eraser to make sharp lines along them. Details that did not look dark enough were filled in with charcoal. The table top was rightly the brightest part of the drawing, but the corner in reality was less bright than the rest, so I rubbed in a light layer of charcoal with the residue on a used paper stump. This also had the effect of having a crescent of light to the left of the drawing. At this point I considered the drawing finished as I had created the feeling of light entering a room.

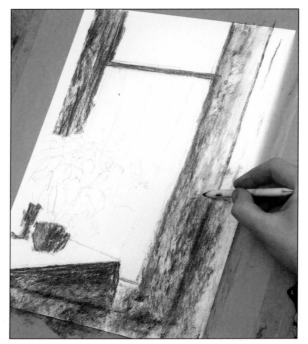

Working the first charcoal layer.

Drawing in the darkest sections with a bamboo pen.

The net curtains put in using a round-ended brush.

Highlighting the edges with a sharpened eraser.

Further ideas

Window scenes like this make good subjects. They do not involve going outside and being exposed to the elements; you can set yourself up comfortably; there are usually several suitable objects around the window for you to draw; and you always have varied light effects. Try similar drawings, say at night or showing the view through the windows.

Window at night

Set yourself up in the same position as you used for the full view of the window. Make sure that the curtains are drawn back so that you can see the reflections in the window. If there is a reflection of yourself there, don't be modest but put it in the drawing! This time you should aim to create a drawing using mixed media that shows the relationship between the window's reflection and the window frame.

First, get the basic framework of your drawing correct by measurement, then build the major tonal relationship before you become involved with the smaller details. By combining wet and dry materials you will be able to achieve different textures and depths.

Near and far

You can also make a drawing through the window into the distance. If you would like to try the idea, you should take up the position you were in for the partial view of the window, except that you may have to be slightly higher so as to have a clear view out of the window.

A variety of mixed media materials will be necessary to do justice to the variety of the subject matter. Accurate measurement is essential to create a recession of scale and size into the background. Try using a different format of paper; for example, a thin rectangular piece. Focus on the smaller shapes in the background and show them with clarity. The objects within the room should be drawn in simple line and tone.

Project: Using a sketchbook

You will need
- a sketchbook
- 2B, 4B and 6B pencils
- a plastic eraser
- a sharp craft knife
  or Stanley knife

A sketchbook is your portable studio; use it whenever you do not have the time for a formal session of drawing. A sketchbook is essential for all visual artists. When you are on holiday, take it with you so that you can make studies wherever you go. The opportunities for using a sketchbook are limitless: draw out of the window of a train; draw while you are waiting in an airport lounge; draw the people you see in your local park. This will give you some practice and you will also teach yourself to observe intuitively.

Sketchbooks are available in a variety of sizes and formats; some are only pocket-sized, while others can be 60cm (2ft) wide or more. It is important to buy a sketchbook with a hardback and strong bindings that make it durable. The paper used in most sketchbooks is light cartridge (drawing), try to find one with at least this quality of paper. A sketchbook measuring about 20 × 15cm (8 × 6in.) is a convenient size.

The length of time you spend on drawings in your sketchbook should be varied. Try to make as many short studies, taking up to two minutes, as long ones.

You should occasionally use odd materials – ballpoint pens, fibre tips or stubby pencils; even draw with a stick dipped in ink or anything else that comes to hand. A change of materials can very often release inhibitions that have blocked your artistic development. The sketchbook is your secret world, and there is no such thing as a mistake in it.

J.M.W. Turner, detail from the sketchbook 'Hesperides I'.

Producing a study

This exercise and the following may lead you to question your own ideas on perception. They may also instinctively become a part of the way you draw. Equally, you should never be afraid to develop existing methods in creating your own drawings.

However, before embarking on more complex drawings in your sketchbook, try some experimental exercises using intuitive observation. Keep an open mind; this is a chance to be rash, to make instinctive marks, and to exaggerate the methods and techniques that you have learned.

Working from observation, make a continuous line drawing of a figure or object, keeping your

The completed study of a figure in pencil.

The shoulders, jacket and bed. Detail.

The basic framework.

hand moving constantly as you look at the subject. This will help you to ensure the line is unbroken. You should try to get the proportions of the composition correct. You can use any materials you like to make the studies and vary the length of time you take.

Another good exercise is to make a series of line drawings of figures or objects. Do not look at your drawing after you have started – just look at the object and try to create the shape and line by intuition. Again you can use any materials you like, but make these studies in under a minute.

Study of a figure

A typical subject that I would want to sketch is a figure relaxing at home. People usually stay fairly still for between 15 and 30 minutes while watching television or reading. If they do make slight movements, I draw over my original lines; I frequently find this enhances the drawing, creating an animated quality. If the figure changes

position, be patient. I often have a series of positions drawn on different pages in my sketchbook. We are all creatures of habit, so a position or postures may well be repeated. If so, I can simply continue with the drawing.

I always try to look at the whole figure and in relation to its surrounding. I draw intuitively in lines of different strengths as I move around and across the shapes, constantly scanning the figure. I never measure – my sketchbook is a place for exploring instinctive marks. For this reason do not use an eraser to make changes.

Head, shoulders and pillows

The model was lying down on some pillows, watching television. I started from where the forehead and edge of the pillow met. I drew the outline of the pillow looking constantly at the subject, not at the paper. I observed the space between the pillow and the head. At first I used tentative light marks; then I worked round and across the forms. As I became more confident about the correctly plotted positions and crucial angles, I made darker marks and lines.

Shoulders, jacket and bed

I jumped from the point of the chin and marked an angle for the collar of the jacket; drawing with flowing lines the creases and folds of the jacket. I looked at the space between the figure and the outside of the bed, and drew it in outline.

A detail of the figure's head.

The head

Then I went back to drawing the head. I looked at the proportions of the nose and cheekbones, and worked from mark to mark: lips to chin, lips to eyes, cheekbone to neck. I made tentative, light marks to indicate these points in space. As I grew more confident of the positions, I made lines and angles. As I was drawing these marks, the model changed position. The drawing was unfinished but it had been excellent practice and I could always continue with a study of a different position.

A walk with my sketchbook

Whenever I go out with my sketchbook, it is a visual adventure. One of my favourite walks takes me to the River Thames, about a mile from my home in Chiswick, London. You too may have a walk that you particularly enjoy, so you can combine this with a sketchbook project. You will be surprised what ordinary things you may have taken for granted, and how much you can enjoy drawing on your way. I decided to make six 10-minute studies on my way to the river and one of 30 minutes, when I reached my destination. I would draw objects in the local environment en route and finally a landscape. I wrote a commentary on the sketches I made as I went along; I described the last drawing – the landscape sketch – in a step-by-step sequence.

A terraced house.

Terraced house

Outside my house I made a quick drawing of my front door and balcony window. I drew the door frame and columns in pencil carefully. The decorative ironwork of the balcony made an intricate pattern against the window. I suggested the brickwork with horizontal lines at regular intervals. I drew the dustbins (trash cans) at odd angles to contrast with the rectangular doorway.

Bicycles against a stand.

Bicycles

I walked to the end of my road, where there was a group of bicycles propped against their stands. Standing a few paces away, I started to draw a single bicycle in relation to its stand.

I drew the frame first. Working instinctively, not using measurement, I kept the pencil on the page almost continuously. The wheels were a series of circular lines. The shape of the stand helped to give the feeling of a bicycle leaning against a stand. The essence of all sketchbook work is spontaneity, so work quickly!

Shop window

Turning off the main road and down a side street towards the river was a row of small shops. The display of fresh fish and shellfish arranged in a window was tempting. I looked at the patterns created by the different seafood and decided to draw a lobster. Flowing pencil lines seemed right for the curvaceous subject, varying the intensity and width of line. I tried to contrast the simple shape of the lobster against the rest of the fish on display around it.

Tree

At the end of the street there was a large roundabout. Struggling amidst the mass of road and cars was a number of trees. I chose one with a simple shape and drew it from the trunk towards its tapering branches, trying hard to follow the exact direction of the shape of the trunk. This was so as to capture the sense of energy rising up the tree from the ground that attracted me to it in the first place. I used light lines and marks, redrawing in heavier lines if I thought that the width or direction of the branches was wrong.

Trees are excellent linear subject matter, because their complex shape and often constant movement are difficult to draw. If you persevere and draw many of them in your sketchbook, it will enhance your skill with line.

Roof top

Then I turned down another side street and looked up at the architectural features of the houses. A chimney and part of the roof stood out against the sky. The rectangular shape of the chimney was drawn first, with the angle of the roof. I drew the chimney pots in line, trying to get their shape and convoluted outline, then quickly toned in the shape of the pots to create contrast.

Churchyard

Walking down the small, winding road I came to a churchyard and noticed a large decorative tomb. It bore an inscription: 'William Hogarth, a painter of moral tales'. Above the inscription was a charming, small stone relief. For an artist, this was irresistible. I drew it in outline, paying special attention to the overlapping features of the relief. The short study took less than 10 minutes to do.

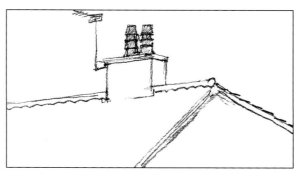

A roof top.

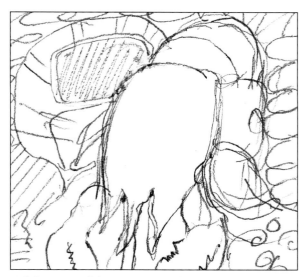

A lobster in a fishmonger's window.

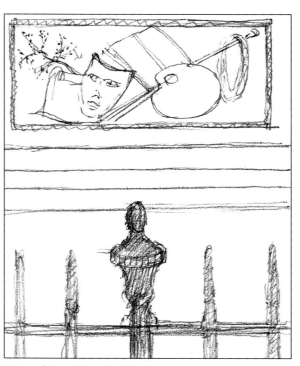

A tree against an urban landscape.

Hogarth's tomb and railings.

The river

Basic structure

Now I was at the river, I chose a subject for the longer, 30-minute sketch. Riversides are never short of interesting subject matter, so the only difficulty in selecting this barge and roadside view was the variety of choice.

Working quickly in pencil, I drew a line bisecting the page in my sketchbook for the edge of the road, in front of the river. Drawing the line of the quay with the moored barge came next. The pencil moved constantly, with my eyes flicking from paper to scene rapidly.

The author drawing the river.

Fence, barge, signs and trees

Next I decided to draw the fence-posts, starting with the farthest one, as all the others would get larger as they came closer to me. Not wanting to make decisions about the tonal balance of the sketch yet, I just drew them in. The signs came next. I was trying to guess distances without measuring, jumping from point to point making marks and lines, so as to maintain the spontaneity. I varied the strength of marks when an object or angle seemed important. Lastly, I drew in the straight line for the height of the river and the edge of the boat, which meant that the basic shapes were established.

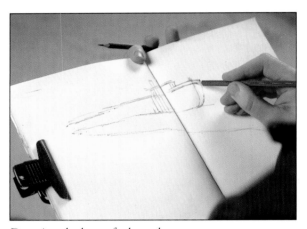

Drawing the bow of a houseboat.

The river

The afternoon light created rippled flowing lines on the surface of the river. I echoed this flow, making my pencil glide across the surface of the paper. Twisting and curling the pencil lines, I tried to create the impression of the slowly receding tide before me.

Contrast

I decided the fence-posts needed contrast against the surface of the river so I made them dark in tone. I also conveyed their haphazard placement by drawing the poles between them which were at odd angles. The surface of the road had random

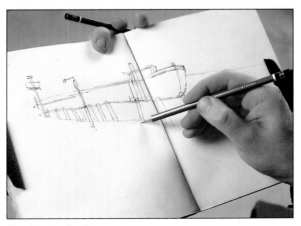

Putting in the fence-posts.

68

patterns; I drew these in short strokes and curved lines. I also drew in the shore and pavement.

Human scale

While I was drawing, a bearded, bohemian painter set up an easel near me and started to paint vigorously. I added his rotund outline and the line of his portable easel. The figure gave the drawing a human scale. Never be afraid to add animals or people to your pencil studies, if they appear while you are drawing; they add a spontaneous touch. One of the great problems of drawing outdoors affected me then: it began to rain so I stopped the drawing and began to walk home.

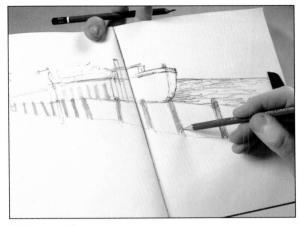

Using pencil to create contrast.

Adding another artist painting to give human scale to the drawing.

PART TWO

Starting in
Watercolour

Introduction

Watercolour painting has a long and living tradition. There are paintings in watercolour in the caves at Altamira and at Lascaux, making it likely that this is the earliest method used by man to record his existence. From that time, people from almost all cultures – including the ancient Egyptians, the Chinese, and the European and English masters of the eighteenth century – have taken the tradition, added to it and developed it. Today, the popularity of watercolour, even in the face of more modern alternatives, seems undiminished, and certainly it is a medium which still attracts many beginners to painting every year.

Watercolour is often called the 'English' medium, although English landscape art really developed from the Dutch school of painting – the two countries are, after all, very close to one another. The topographical artists in England – who were trying to make accurate records of what they saw, usually landscapes, and architectural and botanical drawings – drew their subjects, and then stained them lightly in watercolour, normally pale brown or green. The Dutch influence encouraged a more painterly approach. The French, and through them, the Italian landscape schools also played a part in the development of English watercolour art.

There are many reasons why watercolour painting flourished in Britain around 1800. The Industrial Revolution meant that more people had more money, but it was also a time when people of culture started to travel widely – the 'grand tour' became an essential part of a gentleman's education – and they began to collect works of art. Thomas Gainsborough and Paul Sandby were just two of the great artists who started the Royal Academy and who were instrumental in encouraging collecting, and the vogue for amateur painting. At about this time, there was a large number of gifted and enthusiastic artists using watercolour as a creative medium. The Royal Society of Painters in Water-Colours was formed in London in 1804. Watercolour painting in America owed a great deal to European art in the nineteenth century. In this century, however, a strong national style has developed. As well as producing some brilliant professional artists, the American interest in watercolour painting has encouraged amateur artists and the number of amateur painters in watercolour has increased enormously over the last twenty or thirty years.

Paul Sandby 'Windsor Castle: the Round Tower' 290 × 510mm (11½ × 20½in.). Some of Sandby's most interesting works are his numerous drawings of Windsor Castle. This example is one of his best; it is transparent watercolour over pencil and is a good example of topographical painting in which the drawing predominates.

Charles Bartlett 'Fishing Boats' 350 × 425mm (14 × 17in.). An example of the use of transparent watercolour where the drawing is established by shapes of colour.

This section of *Art Class* is designed to help those people who want to know how to paint in watercolour. It illustrates basic principles and techniques from which you can develop your own approach to the subject and your own personal style. Equipment and materials are listed with advice as to what is necessary and most suitable for the beginner, and through practical instruction you are encouraged to carry out specific projects and exercises. If you follow the guidelines and advice given and work systematically through the projects, by the time you reach the end, you should be able to produce satisfying and technically adept paintings.

For me one of the great charms of watercolour painting is its fluidity and transparency, which can produce a beauty which is unique. I find the spontaneous quality, the simplicity and ability to express mood and light suits my expression as an artist. But one has to be careful that the medium and technique don't become all important; first and foremost one is an artist with something to express.

I believe that the beginner in watercolour is best advised not to spend years learning the academics of drawing first, but rather to start painting and let the drawing develop alongside. They should run hand in hand. Drawing and observation are fundamental to painting and will improve with practice. Enjoy your painting, paint what you know and love best and don't worry too much about what other people say or think.

There are three main styles of watercolour painting. The watercolour drawing (below left) is the traditional use of the medium (as used by the great topographical artists). The drawing in pen or pencil tends to predominate, and the colour is applied in light transparent washes simply to tint the drawing. Watercolour painting (which is the method of painting mostly dealt with here) relies on transparent washes of colour laid over white or pale paper. Some drawing is indicated but the painting is largely colour against colour (right). Gouache (or body colour, below) is the use of opaque watercolour. Its consistency, opacity and visible texture make it different from the more traditional use of watercolours.

Materials and equipment

There are three basic essentials for painting in watercolours – paper (usually called the support), paints and brushes. However, as you will see from the descriptions below (and as a visit to a reputable art supplier will show you), there is a wide range of choice in each of these items. In this section, all the materials and equipment you are likely to come across are considered and the major differences between them discussed.

Paper

Paper is available in a large variety of sizes, weights, qualities and colours, but white or lightly toned papers are the most useful for watercolour. The best papers are hand made from pure linen rags. Mould–made papers are cheaper and quite satisfactory as long as they are made from linen or cotton rags.

    Paper comes in three different finishes: Hot-pressed, Cold-pressed (or 'Not', meaning simply not Hot-pressed) and Rough. The surface of

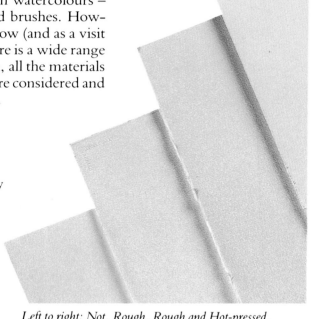

Left to right: Not, Rough, Rough and Hot-pressed.

PAPER TEXTURE

Smooth Hot-Pressed 140lb (295gsm) paper. This paper is the most delicate and sensitive, it is lovely to draw on and probably the most useful for watercolour drawing. It is, however, difficult to control large washes on it and dark colours often go patchy.

Medium Not 140lb (295gsm) paper. This surface has enough texture to produce a delicate painting but also the ability to break up the paint and give crispness in handling. This paper takes washes well and is probably the paper most often used by watercolour artists.

Hot-pressed paper is the smoothest and most absorbent, so this type of paper is less suitable for the transparent watercolour technique than either Not or Rough, both of which take a wash more easily. Not is a textured semi-rough paper which is good for large smooth washes, yet it will also take fine brush detailing. Rough paper is rough textured, and a wash will not always fill the crevices in the surface, presenting a slightly speckled effect. It lends itself to dry-brush techniques (see pages 104-5), but it is difficult to paint fine details on this type of paper. For these reasons Not and Rough are the two most favoured surfaces for watercolour painting; Hot-pressed is more suitable for, and used more often for, drawing or pen work.

Paper is graded by weight, either by pounds per ream (500 sheets) or grams per square metre (gsm). The most common weights available are 72lb (150gsm), 90lb (185gsm) and 140lb (295gsm). Generally, the larger the painting you intend to do, the heavier the paper you use should be, so 72lb (150gsm) is suitable for small paintings and

Paper sizes		
Double Elephant	686 × 1001mm	(27 × 40in.)
A1	594 × 840mm	(24 × 36in.)
A2	420 × 594mm	(18 × 24in.)
Imperial	559 × 762mm	(22 × 30in.)
½ Imperial	381 × 559mm	(22 × 15in.)
Royal	490 × 610mm	(19½ × 25in.)

sketches, 90lb (185gsm) for moderate sized works, and 140lb (295gsm) is necessary for larger works. Traditional Imperial sizes are retained in Britain and the United States for better quality hand- and mould-made papers. For other papers, including cartridge (drawing), the international 'A' sizes (see page 20) are more common.

I use 90lb (185gsm) and 140lb (295gsm) paper, usually Not surface, although occasionally for larger works I use Rough surface. I buy Imperial sheets and cut them down if necessary to the size I require. I find I usually have to stretch the paper (see page 78). This is because once you put a wash on a sheet of paper, the water will make the fibres stretch so the paper will wrinkle and become bumpy. You cannot get a smooth wash on a wavy surface. The heavier grades of paper do show less tendency to wrinkle, particularly in fairly small sizes, so if you are going to do a small painting and not get the sheet too wet, the paper will not need stretching. Certainly anything less than 140lb (295gsm) should always be stretched.

Always be careful to use the right side of the paper; the watermark if held up to the light reads correctly on the side to paint on. Stretch a larger piece of paper than you think you will need, as this will give you some room to manoeuvre over your composition. Sometimes you may want to add a bit on one side or the other to make a better arrangement.

Blocks and pads of watercolour paper are useful, particularly if you are travelling light, but wherever possible I do prefer to buy my paper in sheets and stretch it myself.

Rough 140lb (295gsm) paper. The surface is very coarse and this gives a broken effect to the paint, often making it rather 'jumping' and lively. This surface is not suitable for delicate subjects and lends itself to large paintings.

STRETCHING PAPER

Trim the paper to size. It should be at least 50mm (2in.) smaller all round than the board you intend to stretch it on to. Make sure you use stout board – not one made from thin plywood or hardboard (Masonite). Check the paper for the watermark, when it reads correctly you have the paper right side up. Cut four pieces of 40mm (1½in.) gummed paper strip, one for each side.

Sponge both sides of the paper – wrong side first – with lukewarm water. Warm water softens the size in the paper faster than cold, but don't have the water too hot or you could break down the fibres in the paper. Apply the water gently in case you damage the surface of the paper. Use a full sponge but don't over-saturate the paper. Lay out the damp paper in the correct position on the board.

Press out any air bubbles that form gently from the middle to the edge of the paper with a clean rag. Allow the paper to relax for about five minutes (for 90lb/185gsm – allow up to ten for 140lb/295gsm). Wet the lengths of gumstrip, and lay them around the edges of the paper, allowing approximately equal overlap between the paper and board. Rub the gumstrip well down.

Place drawing pins through the gumstrip and paper at each corner to ensure that the paper lies flat. Allow the paper to dry naturally in a horizontal position (this will take a few hours or overnight). The stretching will be spoiled if you use artificial heat. Once it is completely dry, the paper is ready to use.

Brushes

Brushes are the most personal tool an artist uses. For this reason, buy the best you can afford – it is better to have one or two good-quality brushes than several indifferent ones. The best watercolour brushes are, unfortunately (but not surprisingly), the most expensive. They are made from red sable hair, and are soft, springy and very well set in the ferrule. They also hold a lot of water (which makes them ideal for washes) and the hairs always go to a good point. Less expensive natural-hair brushes are made from either ox hair or camel hair. Ox hair is more springy than sable and tougher, but it does not hold so much water or produce such a fine point. Camel hair (actually usually squirrel) is relatively cheap, but it does not have the spring or life of either sable or ox hair, and the hairs often tend to come out of the ferrule. There is also a range of watercolour brushes on the market that combine synthetic fibre with a proportion of sable. These are superior to camel hair and cheaper than natural hair and can be recommended if you cannot afford pure sable.

Watercolour brushes range in size from the tiny 000 to a size 14. The size is directly related to the number of hairs in the ferrule – a No. 10, for instance, has approximately ten times as many hairs as a No. 1. To begin with, I would suggest you buy one each of Nos 2, 5, 7 and 10.

Good brushes are expensive, but will last a long time if they are properly cared for. Always wash out your brushes in clean water before you finish for the day. If the brush is stained, and clean water alone does not remove the paint, wash it gently with lukewarm water and soap but make sure the brush is well rinsed with clean water afterwards. Shape the brush naturally either between your lips, or by gently shaking the hairs to a point. Do not store brushes until they are completely dry. If a brush is in constant use, store it with its bristles upright in a jam (jelly)-jar or similar container. For longer term storage, they can be kept in a brush container or box with some mothballs.

The marks made by watercolour brushes of different sizes: (left to right) Nos 00, 2, 5, and 10.

79

Paints

The standard of paint manufacture, on the whole, is extremely high and a wide range of colours is now produced. Watercolours are made up of transparent pigments ground extremely finely and mixed with gum. Gouache or designers' colour differs from watercolour in that the colour has precipitated chalk, as well as gum, mixed with it.

Pure watercolour is available in several forms, as dry cakes, semi-moist pans, tubes and bottles of concentrated colour. Dry cakes contain pigment in its purest form; semi-moist pans and tubes usually have glycerine added to keep them moist.

Dry cakes
These are the traditional form of watercolour. The colour in these hard round cakes is pure and is still preferred by some watercolourists. These cakes need more water than pans or tubes to release the colour, and unless they are used regularly, they get very hard and need a lot of scrubbing up.

Pans and half pans
These are small blocks of semi-moist watercolour, which are designed to fit into watercolour boxes which can be purchased separately. You can, therefore, buy the colours individually, making your own selection. Whole pans are slightly more economical, but both offer a strong yield of colour that can be easily worked and diluted. They are very convenient for use out of doors.

Tubes
The colour in tubes is more loosely ground and does not dry out provided the tubes are re-sealed after use. Tubed watercolour is convenient for squeezing out large amounts and is instantly workable, it doesn't need 'scrubbing up'. For this reason, it is probably more suitable for use in the studio or on a large-scale painting. A special box or container is not necessary to hold the tubes – a plastic bag will suffice – and a white plate makes a good palette.

Tubes and pans of watercolour are available in Artists' quality or Students' quality, Students' quality generally being about one-quarter of the price of Artists' quality. All reputable paint manufacturers grade their products according to durability and permanence. Winsor and Newton, for example, classify their Artists' watercolours in four grades of permanence: Class AA Extremely durable; Class A Durable; Class B Moderately durable; and Class C Fugitive. The durability and permanence of Artists' colours should be checked against the manufacturer's colour list – do not select colours which are fugitive.

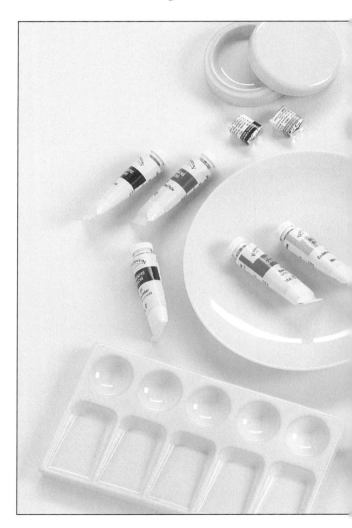

Some of the pigments used in Artists' quality paints are expensive and this is reflected in the price. However, I would recommend you buy the best available materials; in this case, Artists' quality paints. It is a mistake to think anything will do – you will only add to any problems.

Palettes and paintboxes

The watercolour box usually has white enamelled recesses for mixing colour, this is the most convenient form of carrying and using semi-moist watercolours, particularly for outdoor work.

If you are using tube colours you will need well palettes or pots. A conventional kidney-shaped palette is very useful but it must be white and have recesses for mixing colour.

If you are buying a paintbox (or having one for a gift) it is better to choose one that is not too small, say with spaces for about 12 or 14 pans. It should have large mixing pans and clips for holding the pans so that they can be changed. A box with a thumb-hole or ring is easier to hold. Also, buy the paints separately from the paintbox. In this way, you can select colours to suit you and your style of working.

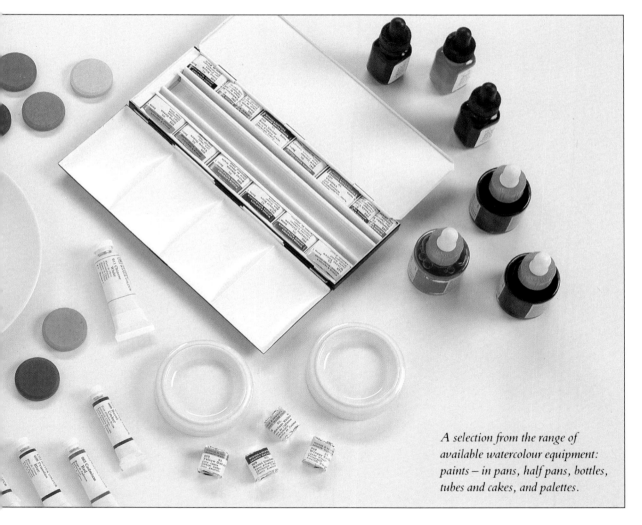

A selection from the range of available watercolour equipment: paints – in pans, half pans, bottles, tubes and cakes, and palettes.

Artists' furniture

Stools

If you are working out of doors a good folding stool is very useful but make sure it is strong and reasonably comfortable. A stool which is too small or too low can mean you get terrible cramp, often just when you have reached a critical point in your watercolour. There are some good light aluminium (aluminum) stools on the market.

Folding table

If you are working at home and have to pack your gear away after use, a folding table is necessary, unless of course you are fortunate enough to have a studio. There are drawing tables (some of which are used in schools) with adjustable angled boards and drawers but the better quality ones do not fold away. An ordinary 1.25m (4ft) wooden folding table is adequate.

Easels

Although an easel is not essential, it is very useful, if for no other reason than it leaves both your hands free. It needs to be the folding type for outdoor work and must be stable and light. There is a three-legged easel on the market which has a pivoting main shaft that can be swung either vertically or horizontally. This makes it useful for standing or sitting to work. Easels are made from wood or aluminium, both of which are reasonably light and satisfactory.

Drawing boards

These really fall into two categories, the one to be used at home or in the studio and the one used for sketching and outdoor work. In the former case weight doesn't matter too much so a good solid ½ Imperial board is what is required (or full Imperial if you have room). For outdoor work it is probably best to make a drawing board out of exterior plywood, in fact make several of different sizes: 38 × 56cm (15 × 22in.), 28 × 38cm (11 × 15in.) and 38 × 45cm (15 × 18in.). You can use

An easel with a pivoting main shaft enables you to stand or sit to work so is probably the most versatile buy, though table top ones are also available.

them to stretch paper on both sides if you get the ply thick enough (otherwise it will bow under the strain of the stretched paper). Use plywood that is at least 7mm (⅜in.) thick for a board 38 × 56cm (15 × 22in.) – it can be thinner for smaller sizes.

Other useful equipment

Sponges of all sizes are useful for dampening a small area, washing off a small area of paint, or painting or creating a texture. You will also need one large one for sponging and stretching paper. Natural sponge is better than synthetic.

Soft cotton rags are useful for wiping your brushes on.

Absorbent paper tissues of any kind can be used for mopping out colour, or correcting a watercolour. It is also possible to create texture with them (see page 104).

A toothbrush is useful for splatter work. The toothbrush is dipped in paint and then a knife is drawn across the bristles; this causes fine splatter or mottling (see page 92).

Cottonwool buds (cotton swabs) are used for mopping out tiny areas of colour, and correcting.

Erasers are necessary for rubbing out pencil or charcoal marks. You will need a vinyl eraser for charcoal, and a soft eraser for pencil. An ink or typewriter eraser can also be useful for taking out small areas of colour.

Pencils are ideal for sketching in lines before painting and planning your paintings, also for making studies and notes. Initially, softer grades are the most useful.

Gummed paper is necessary when you are stretching paper (see page 78) and for sealing the back of frames.

You may find some (or all) of these items useful in your work. Apart from household items like rags, sponges and a toothbrush, you may need a bottle of masking fluid or gum arabic for a particular effect.

Blades, either single-sided razor blades or sharp craft knife blades, are useful for scraping and correcting small areas of paint (see pages 102 and 112). A sharp craft knife is a useful tool for cutting paper and mounts (mats).

Masking fluid protects areas of work when applying washes (see pages 106–7).

Masking tape is necessary in order to fasten paper to boards (although not for stretching paper) and to mask straight lines, for example, the borders of a painting.

Gum arabic is used in the manufacture of watercolour, and is useful to have in the studio for thickening paint and to create a texture.

A palette knife (metal spatula) is a useful implement for spreading paint, particularly gouache, on to paper. It can also be used for moving colour around or for putting small touches of colour into a painting.

Water containers are vital. Plastic bottles with screw tops are the simplest to get hold of, but specially made containers for watercolour painting are available on the market. These have a top which can be clipped on to your paintbox as a water pot. In the home or studio, jam-jars or plastic bowls are alternatives.

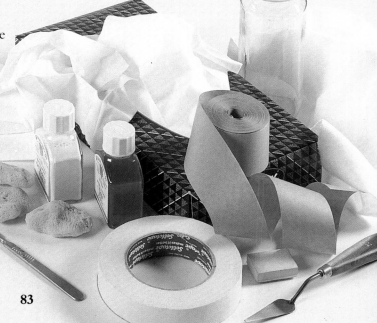

Recommended kit

The items detailed and illustrated here are ones that I consider suitable for a beginner in watercolour. All are readily available and reasonably priced, and with them you should be able to produce good-quality paintings.

Paper Either Arches mould-made Not 90 lb (185 gsm) or T.H. Saunders Waterford Not 90 lb (185 gsm). Both of these papers are ideal for a beginner since they take washes well, yet are sufficiently robust to allow you to sponge out areas you don't like. You should stretch either of these papers before you use it unless you are simply carrying out a small exercise. Both of these papers are readily available from artists' suppliers.

Paints You should have a watercolour box containing the following colours in semi-moist whole or half pans of Artists' quality colours: cadmium yellow, yellow ochre, raw sienna, raw umber, burnt umber, light red, cadmium red, viridian, cobalt blue, prussian blue, alizarin crimson, and neutral tint. Chinese white may also be useful. With these colours you can mix almost any shade for still-life or landscape painting.

Brushes Nos 2, 5, 7 and 10. The No. 10 could be either ox hair or synthetic as a sable brush this size would be very expensive.

Additional items A ½ Imperial (22 × 15in.) drawing board, either bought or home made; pencils (grades B and 2B); some sticks of vine charcoal; a soft pencil eraser and a vinyl eraser; an easel and stool; water containers – jam-jars or plastic bowls will do; a sponge; some cotton rags; and a sketching bag (to keep all your equipment in – this is more important for work outdoors).

You don't need a vast array of materials and equipment to start painting in watercolour. The main items you are likely to need to carry out the exercises and projects in this section are illustrated here.

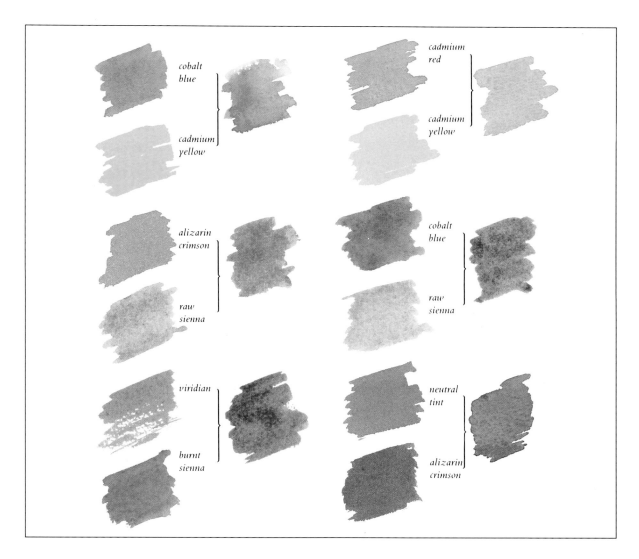

Colour mixing

To mix a colour, first put some clean water into your palette or container, then take a clean brush, moisten it and dip just the point into your selected colour and mix this with the brush into the prepared water on the palette. To vary this colour, make sure your brush is clean, then dip it into the second colour and mix with the original wash.

Make marks on a sheet of paper of all the colours you use and mix. Write against these colour splurges the correct name of the colour you are using, and the colour you make; for example,

cobalt blue + cadmium yellow = green, or cadmium yellow + cadmium red = orange. Cover a sheet of paper with these little exercises and you will begin to learn more about how colours look when mixed with one another.

The more colours you mix together, the greater your chances of producing a muddy brown, so initially at least limit yourself to mixing two or three colours. Also, always make sure that you have plenty of clean water available, at least one container for cleaning your brush and one for use in making your colour.

Starting to paint

Watercolour painting relies on transparent washes of colour laid over a reflecting light-toned paper (unlike gouache which has white mixed with the colour and so can be painted on any coloured paper). This means that to paint successfully in watercolour you must master the basic technique of laying a wash. For any area you wish to paint which is too large for a simple brush stroke a wash is necessary.

In all successful paintings a satisfactory composition depends upon simple flat areas (washes) being played against complex areas. One only has to study a watercolour by John Sell Cotman or David Hockney to realize the importance of a flat wash. If you start by mastering this technique it will give confidence and lead you into both the fun and the mystery of watercolour painting. It is a bit like learning scales if you want to play the piano, both need a lot of practice. After you have bought the equipment suggested on page 84, take and stretch several pieces of watercolour paper – for these experiments they do not have to be very big, about 25 × 30cm/10 × 12in. should be large enough – and practise laying washes as described opposite.

You will need
☐ a drawing board with stretched paper
☐ two jars of clean water
☐ paints
☐ brushes
☐ a white plate or palette
☐ a stick of charcoal
☐ a soft pencil and eraser
☐ masking fluid
☐ razor or craft knife blades

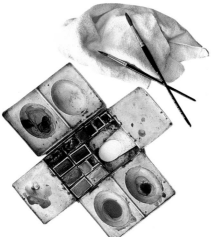

This paintbox is well designed: it has a thumbhole for ease of holding, there are four deep mixing pans, spaces for ten whole pans of paint, and it is robust, yet not too heavy.

The author in his studio, showing details of worktop and watercolour equipment. Normally, work is done on the workbench but it is useful when putting finishing touches to a painting to use an easel; it enables you to stand back from the work.

Flat washes

A flat wash is an even distribution of transparent watercolour, and laying one is the basic technique of all pure watercolour painting. There is something very seductive and beautiful about a lovely watercolour wash.

To mix the colour for the wash, first put a quantity of water into your container (for large washes separate porcelain stacking palettes/cabinet nests are very useful). The quantity will vary according to the area you wish to cover but on an average start with about a small egg cup (4 tablespoons) of water. Add the colour by moistening your brush and with the point lifting the paint from the pan. The more paint you add to the water, the more intense the colour will be but remember that the watercolour will always dry lighter than it looks when it is applied. It is easier to lay a flat wash on a Rough or Not surfaced paper and if the area you wish to cover is fairly large and simple it will help your wash if you dampen the paper first. (If you were painting around small shapes, this would not be possible.)

Use as large a brush as possible, depending upon the complexity of the area. Keep the board tilted at about a 30 degree angle and start at the top of the sheet with a well-loaded brush. Continue backwards and forwards horizontally, working left to right and right to left down your paper.

Work systematically at the speed the wash runs, so that you always pick up the band of colour that is forming at the bottom of the stroke. This means that if you are working with a very watery wash you will have to work faster than if you are using a wash with a higher proportion of colour in it.

When you arrive at the bottom of your paper you will find a surplus pool of colour gathering. Mop this up with a squeezed out brush or sponge. If you don't, you will find the colour running back on itself as it dries and spoiling the flatness of your wash. If the wash does go blotchy, let it dry completely, then with a clean sponge and water gently sponge it down.

LAYING A FLAT WASH

Mix plenty of colour, more than you think you'll need.

Lay strokes alternately left to right and right to left.

Pick up the pool of colour from the previous brush stroke.

Graduated washes

A graduated (or graded) wash is one that starts with intense saturated colour at the top, then progresses through carefully controlled tonal gradations to a colour so pale that it merges with the colour of the paper at the bottom.

Dampen the paper. Start by mixing plenty of colour, remembering that the paint will dry several shades lighter than it appears when wet. When you are satisfied with the colour, load a brush with full strength paint and lay a stroke of colour across the top of the paper, working quickly. Your board should be tilted so that a stream of wash gathers along the bottom of the band of colour. Next dip the brush into the container of clean water, and without adding more paint to the brush lay another stroke of colour under the first, making sure that you pick up the fluid paint along the base of the previous stroke. Repeat this process until you reach the bottom of the sheet of paper. The wash will gradually get weaker until it merges with the colour of the paper.

Mop up any excess paint which has accumulated at the bottom of the paper, then allow the paint to dry, leaving the board tilted at about a 30 degree angle so that the wet colour does not flow back over the dry colour.

LAYING A GRADUATED WASH

Start at the top with full strength colour.

Add increasing amounts of water as you progress.

This simple painting relies on graduated and variegated washes. The sky is a graded wash of blue and the strokes of yellow and mauve make a variegated wash at the horizon.

88

Variegated washes

The term variegated wash usually means two or three colours, rather than tones of a single colour, being merged together. Dampen your paper first using either a sponge or a large brush and clean water, as this will help the colours to merge. Mix your three colours in separate containers. They do not all have to be of the same consistency; you could, for example, make one more intense by using more colour and less water.

Starting at the top of the sheet of paper, paint a strip of your first colour (as if you were laying a flat wash). Quickly, while this is still wet, lay a strip of your second colour, then repeat this with your third. The edges of the colour will spread out and melt into one another. Whatever you think of the initial result, leave the wash well alone until it is completely dry. Additions or corrections can be made then.

Only experience will tell you how much colour you may need and the result will always be rather unpredictable, but practice will help. Changing the tilt of the board can also help you control the merging of the colours. If the board is kept flat, the colours will spread out into each other; as you increase the tilt of the board, the upper layers of wash will run down and melt and merge into the lower ones.

LAYING A VARIEGATED WASH

The first colour merges into the second.

The second colour will then merge into the third.

The sea is a graded wash in reverse; that is, it starts at the horizon with a pale wash, and increasing amounts of colour are added as it reaches the bottom.

Wet into wet

'Wet into wet' implies laying wet paint on a wet surface; in this way, the technique is very similar to laying variegated washes in that the second colour you add spreads and merges into the first.

Watercolour relies for its charm upon its transparency and freshness and a lot of this effect can best be achieved by a wet-into-wet technique, particularly in the early stages of painting. While the wash is still wet, areas can be lifted out with blotting paper or a squeezed out sponge or brush, and edges can also be softened. Artists usually work a stiffer, more intense colour into the wet surface of a pale colour. Try to create some of the effects in the exercises on these two pages yourself – they were all achieved by adding wet paint to wet paint. Wet into wet involves a good degree of the unknown, and hence leaves room for the happy accident – perhaps that is the gambling instinct coming out in the artist! Having said that, experimenting with these techniques will give you the familiarity with what watercolour will do to enable you to control the paint. Do not be worried by mistakes but be prepared to learn by them.

Right: A pale flat wash of prussian blue was put over the whole surface, and while this was still wet I dropped a darker blob of the same colour into the centre and allowed it to spread. I then dabbed another blob of darker thicker colour into the middle and before it could be allowed to spread too much, I lifted out some of the colour with a squeezed out brush.

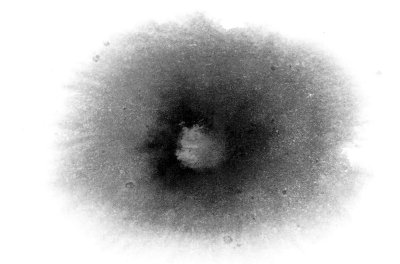

Below right: A pale wash of raw sienna was put over the whole surface, and before it was completely dry random brush strokes of prussian blue were added. Unless the surface is dried off fairly rapidly, the whole will merge together and the effect will be lost. This technique can be useful for cloud effects or foliage.

Far right: A wash of raw sienna was put over the whole surface, and before it was completely dry I applied a squiggle of drier light red very rapidly. This merged in places. This technique is unpredictable but can achieve unexpectedly interesting results.

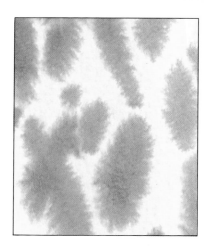

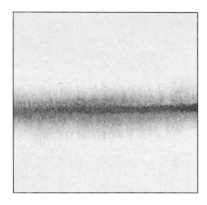

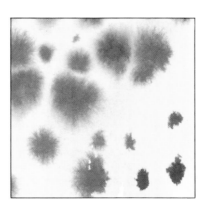

Far left: A wash of cadmium yellow was put over the whole surface, and while this was still wet, I drew a single brush stroke across the middle using a rather thick mixture of indigo. If you don't want the second colour to spread too widely, dry off the paint in front of a fire or radiator, or use a hairdryer, but keep the dryer well away from the paint surface or it will move the colour (see page 102).

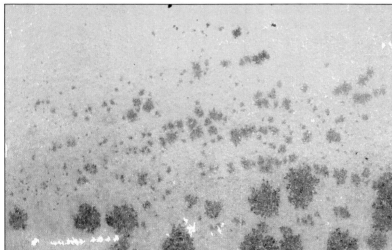

Left above: A thin wash of cadmium yellow was put over the whole surface and because the board was kept at an angle, the top started to dry first. I then touched the surface in spots with just the tip of a brush loaded with prussian blue. Where the paper was damper the spots spread wider; the ones near the bottom right hardly spread at all.

Left: This is a graduated wash of raw sienna to which increasing quantities of light red were gradually added. Before this was completely dry, prussian blue was splattered (see page 92) from the bottom upwards. The dots tend to be bigger the nearer they are to the toothbrush, and again the wash is wetter at the lower edge.

Left: This technique is not easy to control but it is used a lot by artists. A horizontal stripe of cadmium yellow was brushed into the top and while this was still wet a similar stripe of prussian blue laid next to it. The two merged together. The third colour (burnt sienna, with a little light red added) was added while the other two colours were still wet; this then also merged with the prussian blue.

Wet into dry

Working 'wet into dry' – that is, putting wet paint on a layer of paint that has dried, or on dry paper – gives you the greatest control over the application of paint. The paint can be applied direct to the white paper or over another colour. Always be sure that one colour is completely dry before putting on a second. To cover an area, apply the paint in the same way as for a wet surface wash, starting at the top and working down the paper from side to side. Make sure that you have mixed enough colour before you start.

When you work wet into dry, the paint does not run as freely as it does when you work wet into wet because of the resistance of the paper to the paint. This can be useful, however, as it gives the colour a sparkling effect which you don't get when you work wet into wet, because the colours blur. Wet-into-dry techniques should always be used for painting round intricate shapes, and for painting details.

It is sometimes useful to drag the paint across the paper using a fairly dry colour, or to paint with a quick brush stroke which will often produce a broken effect at the end of the stroke. This effect, which is very typical of the medium, is easier to achieve on a Rough or Not paper.

Splatter

Splatter relies on dots of paint of various sizes for its effect. It is fairly random since you have little control over where the spots of colour will go but it is a useful technique to master.

Dip an old toothbrush or hog hair brush into paint until it is well coated but give it a shake to get rid of surplus liquid. Hold it over the surface of your paper and gently draw a craft knife blade towards you through the bristles. This will create a spray of paint, with larger dots of colour the nearer they are to the brush. When this is completely dry, a second colour can be splattered over the first. Masking tape can be combined with the splattering to create shapes and patterns.

SPLATTERING

Build up colour gradually to avoid blots.

Stippling

This wet-into-dry technique is useful as it is easily controlled and gives a vigorous effect. Modelling of light and shade can be achieved by varying the size of the dots, how closely they are packed together and, of course, by the use of different coloured dots. It is possible to get brighter secondary colours such as green by mixing blue and yellow spots. In this way the colours mix in the spectator's eye at a certain distance to give a brighter and clearer green than one can get by mixing on the palette. This is the basic theory of the Pointillists.

A brush that has lost its point can sometimes be an ideal tool for this technique. Don't get the brush too overloaded with colour or you will find your dots are in danger of running together. Hold the brush nearly vertical and dab the colour on.

If this technique is executed with very fine dots, the painting can come to look like a photograph and in Victorian times artists used it for this very reason. But the science of colour theory as evolved by the Impressionists and Post-Impressionists has given this technique a modern application. Comparing it with splatter, you have more control both on where it goes and over the size of the dots.

I selected this subject for this exercise because it was simple and lent itself well to stippling. The dots on the near foliage and in the foreground are larger and further apart than those behind the house to create a feeling of distance, and a sense of light and shade. For this painting, I used the point of a number 4 sable-haired brush. Do not overload the brush with colour if you intend to try this technique, as the dots may run together.

Project: Painting a still life

A still life is simply an arrangement of inanimate objects. Usually these objects are brought together by the artist, but a still life could also be a collection of items from the corner of a room or on a shelf, or a completely random group of objects or plants. A still life is a good choice of subject for a beginner, since the objects are easily available and tend to be familiar, and because of this, you know their basic structures. When you are arranging a still life for a painting at this stage, don't make it too complicated or include too many colours. Instead, as I have here, select a few objects that have differing textures and whose tones contrast.

You will need
- [ ] a drawing board with stretched paper
- [ ] two jars of clean water
- [ ] paints
- [ ] brushes
- [ ] a white plate or palette
- [ ] a stick of charcoal
- [ ] a soft pencil and eraser
- [ ] a cotton rag
- [ ] a sponge

Preliminary sketches

Set out your work space and start with everything clean. You will need a table on which to lay out your materials and work. Prop your board at about a 30 degree angle to the left-hand side of your table (if you are right-handed) – this will leave space on your right for materials. Work in a good light; it is usually better to have the light source slightly from the left (again, if you are right-handed) although this, of course, is dictated to a certain extent by where you arrange your still-life group. You will need to stretch your paper beforehand (see page 78) so that it is dry by the time you want to start work. For this project, I have used a ½ Imperial sheet of Not 90lb (185gsm) watercolour paper. I would recommend at this stage that you have two stretched pieces of paper ready. You'll find you worry much less about making a mistake and therefore paint in a more relaxed way if you have the freedom to discard a sheet if something goes wrong. Arrange your materials on the right of your board so that you can easily reach your paintbox and the water.

Don't try to produce a painting exactly the same as mine, but use this as a guide to method. I chose the objects for my painting partly for their contrasting textures and tones. The smooth, polished enamel jug and plain flat background are played against the texture of the pears and orange and the movement in the leaves. In choosing and arranging your group of objects you may consider some of the following factors, but don't let these suggestions confuse or intimidate you – skill in composition will grow with experience:

1 the size of the objects – try to vary them;
2 the dominant colour – decide whether you want the finished picture to be warm or cool;
3 try to include some straight lines, and some curved or wriggling shapes;
4 try to have one object that attracts the eye first – this can be achieved by colour, size or definition.

Try several arrangements of your objects and perhaps make several small pencil sketches. These

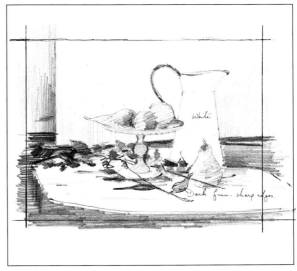

The preliminary sketch to establish composition and tones.

The drawing is sketched in on the stretched paper.

are probably more use if the tones are scribbled in, rather than being in line only. These preliminary sketches are a great help in clarifying the picture in the artist's mind.

Once you have decided on your still-life arrangement, sketch the main lines of your composition on to your sheet of paper with a soft pencil or stick of charcoal.

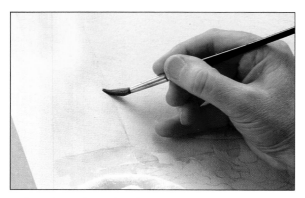

Softening an edge with a clean moist brush.

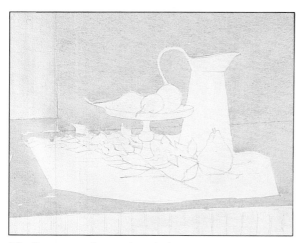

The first two washes on the painting.

The darker wash helps to create a middle tone.

The initial washes

Once you have established the drawing, you are ready to paint. Initially, I laid a flat wash of raw sienna over the whole surface of the paper, apart from the jug, which will be the lightest area of the finished painting. An initial wash of one colour over a large area of the painting like this unifies it and will hold the later colours together. It also gives an overall warmth to the painting, which, because watercolour is a transparent medium, will come through all the later colours to the finished painting.

While the raw sienna wash was still wet, a thin wash of cadmium yellow was flooded into the upper left of the picture and on to the table top. After allowing this to dry completely, I added the warm pink/brown over the table area and the background; this was made up with a mixture of raw sienna and light red with a very little alizarin crimson added. Again this was put on as a flat wash, starting at the top and working down. Before this was dry, to avoid a hard edge between the colours in this part of the painting, I softened the edge of the upright on the left-hand side with a clean moist brush.

At this stage, there are really only two washes on the paper and, with drying time, it probably took me about 15 minutes.

Adding the darker washes

The previous washes had obscured some of the drawing so I strengthened this slightly, although still keeping the lines light – you don't want the drawing to dominate the finished painting. The single darker wash on the table top was added next. This was made up with burnt sienna and light red, and was deliberately not laid too flatly to give a feeling of surface. In any case, it would be overpainted for greater contrast at a later stage.

It is always useful to establish some of these larger washes in a painting first as they help to create a unity of colour (in this case a warm glow). The smaller details and stronger contrasts will be left until later.

Overpainting the darker portions of the fruit stand.

The cool grey shadow helps to create form and space.

The first details

The stand holding the fruit was painted next. This colour was a wash of neat burnt sienna, which was allowed to dry. However, this left the stand without any sense of light and shade, so to create this impression I overpainted the darker portions with another wash of the same colour. I then started on the pears, initially applying a wash of viridian mixed with cadmium yellow. The quince was also painted with a wash, this time made up of a mixture of cadmium yellow and a little cadmium red. While this was still wet, a little of the green used on the pears was gently blended in. I used a wet-into-wet technique in this area to

avoid any harsh contrasts. The softly blurred yellow and green here were intended eventually to contrast with, and complement, both in colour and feeling, the dark, crisply and freshly painted leaves.

At this stage, although I intended the finished painting to be warm, I felt that everything in the picture was getting *too* warm, so I added some cool grey to the upper left-hand side of the picture, deliberately leaving the wash uneven to emphasize the smooth wash of the background. I also used the same colour for the shadow of the quince. The yellow of the foreground was added next – a wash of cadmium yellow.

Applying an initial wash to the pears.

The first details have now been established.

Stippling the pears adds texture.

This completes the painting of the fruit.

The darker leaves are the last details to be painted.

Adding texture

The painting was beginning to appear but was still flat, and so now was the time to give it dimension by adding the textures. The orange was painted with a wash of cadmium yellow and a little cadmium red, which was allowed to dry. I then added more cadmium red to the colour on my palette and painted on this darker colour, leaving small islands of the paler colour showing through to create the impression of the fruit's texture. The darker colour on the pears – a mixture of viridian and raw sienna – was applied with a stipple technique, leaving some of the lighter colour showing through. At this stage too the shadow on the white jug was painted. This was a wash of indigo with a touch of raw sienna added, and while it was still wet, I softened the edge with a clean moist brush to enhance the shadow effect.

The darker details

The darker details will bring the picture to life, so they need to be painted crisply and freshly. For this reason, I have left them until last. The colour for the leaves was made with prussian blue and burnt sienna, which I painted over all the leaves and stalks. Then, to give variety and depth, I created the darker areas by putting a mixture of indigo and viridian wet into wet. I also used a dilute mixture of this colour to paint loosely over the left-hand side of the picture, since I felt that the grey I had previously painted did not bring that area of the picture alive enough.

The final touches

Finishing details are added to sharpen the image, and bring the whole painting together. The blue of the jug handle was cobalt blue and the richer brown on the table was overpainted to give that area more texture and life. The shadow of the quince was then moved. I did this by dampening it with clean water and sponging it down. Finally, I loosely laid a pale green wash in horizontal stripes to indicate the shadows of the leaves, and to help create the horizontal plane of the table.

Mounting (Matting) your work

When the painting is finished, decide where you want the mount (mat) to cut it. A mount defines the boundaries of your painting (and hides the rather untidy edges). Generally, I would suggest you use a 2-sheet white mounting card next to the watercolour with a 4-sheet off-white mounting card 6mm (¼in.) larger laid over the first one. For a painting of this size, margins of about 75mm (3in.) at the top and sides, and 90mm (3½in.) at the bottom will be about right.

Don't forget the old adage: if at first you don't succeed, try try and try again. Watercolour is not an exact medium – there will always be an element of chance about anything you paint. A painting can be going quite well and then suddenly something goes wrong – a colour runs badly, for example, or goes dirty. You can sometimes resurrect a painting in cases like this, but often I find it's best to start again. (This is why I suggest you should have two sheets of paper ready stretched.) I can assure you that all the practice you do will be worth while. As you become increasingly familiar with the medium you will gain in confidence and find that your work is improving.

The finishing details, painted crisply and freshly, bring the painting to life.

Further techniques

The kit of the artist is not confined to just paints and brushes, but blotting paper, sponges, hairdryers and many other household objects have their uses. The applications of these are not intended as tricks – they are part of the genuine vocabulary of the watercolour painter, to be used if and when they are considered necessary to strengthen an image. All painters develop their own techniques; the following demonstrations represent only a small selection of those possible.

This does not mean that you should ever try to use all these techniques in a single painting, any more than it would be advisable to use all the colours in your box on one watercolour. Perhaps you would only use one or two of these techniques in any one painting. I have tried not to include a lot of fringe materials and techniques, because they may just confuse. However do experiment, perhaps try drawing with a stick dipped in watercolour, or use washing–up (dishwashing) liquid to obtain a texture or try scratching a wet colour with the back of your brush. There is no need to use good paper, cartridge (drawing) will do, but just try as many effects as you can devise.

Some artists like using an old-fashioned shaving brush for large washes or even an airbrush. Sometimes in the excitement of making a watercolour you are tempted to try some wonderful techniques like one of these. It might come off, or it might completely ruin your work, but that I'm afraid is the nature of the beast we call watercolour! Do remember, too, that all these techniques are only of use if they help you to express your idea in a stronger way: they are of little or no use as an end in themselves.

You will need
☐ a drawing board with stretched paper
☐ two jars of clean water
☐ paints
☐ brushes
☐ a white plate or palette
☐ blotting paper
☐ natural sponges
☐ masking fluid
☐ razor or craft knife blades
☐ a hairdryer
☐ white candle wax
☐ tissue paper

This sketch (right) is made up of only flat washes and sponged texture. For the three larger trees, I laid a flat wash which I allowed to dry. I then painted some of this same colour on to a natural sponge and gently dabbed the area of the trees – this gives two tones. The darker shadows on these large trees were created by dabbing some of the colour I had mixed for the small tree into the still wet texture. I then just touched some red into this still wet paint to add highlights. The different texture on the small tree was created in exactly the same way but using a finer sponge.

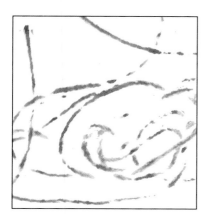 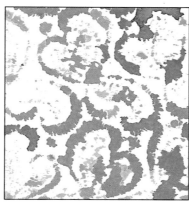

Left: Alternative patterns can be created using string (far left) and lace, pressed into paint and on to paper.

Sponging

Sponging is usually used to add texture to a painting and is a particularly useful technique for adding foliage to trees and bushes, and for creating the impression of greenery (see also pages 110-11). Sponge gives a random, exciting effect, which is not easily produced with a brush. It is a good idea to build up a collection of sponges of different sizes and different degrees of coarseness – also, I find natural sponge far better than synthetic. The area to be textured dictates the size and coarseness of the sponge to use.

For a small area, you can apply the paint to the sponge with a brush, but for larger areas prepare the wash in a saucer or deep palette and dip the sponge in lightly. If you get the sponge too wet, the texture will be almost non–existent. If the sponging is applied to a damp area of paper, it will tend to spread and you will get a softer effect; if the surface is dry, it will give a crisp and much more pronounced texture. A tone or colour can also be darkened by successive dabbing with the colour on the sponge and you can, of course, apply two colours, but again if you want the end result to be a crisp texture, allow the first to dry before applying the second.

Sometimes a wash which is too flat and uninteresting can be brought to life by sponging a light texture on to it. A touch of a dark colour dabbed with a sponge into still wet paint adds a random lively feel to an area of a painting. I achieved the highlights in the picture below by dabbing touches of red into the still wet sponging.

Drying and blowing

Blowing the paint surface while it is still wet spreads the colour, but is very difficult to control, and so is not used very often. Sometimes, you can achieve a happy accident, but I rarely use this method myself.

Lay a flat wash over the whole area, and while it is still wet use a hairdryer close to the surface to blow the paint where you want it to go. As it dries, it tends to granulate the colour, which can be very attractive. You can also blow wet paint through a drinking straw, although this again is a rather random technique.

Controlled drying, on the other hand, can be very useful. If you dry off an area rapidly, the colour doesn't have time to spread or run back on itself. You can use a hairdryer for this too, but don't put it too near the paper surface or you risk moving the paint. I use an electric fire (space-heater) with a guard. It seems to suit my technique better – it also helps me to keep warm in my garden studio! Obviously, you should only use a safe fire that is easy to handle, and be confident that you know what you are doing.

Scratching

If a wash, or succession of washes, has gone dull, or their transparency has been lost, you can bring some life back to the surface by scratching the paint off the pinnacles of the paper's surface texture using a single-sided razor blade or a sharp craft knife blade. If the edge is used, either will give an all-over textured effect; if only the point is applied, it will give a more linear quality. However, it is difficult to put a wash over an area you have scratched as the surface of the paper has been destroyed. Also, this technique is only suitable on a heavyweight paper.

It is also possible to take an area of wash back to the white paper with sandpaper. Use a fine-grained sandpaper and rub in a gentle circular motion at the area of paint you wish to remove. Don't be impatient – take the paint off gradually. Depending on the quality of the paper you use and the area of colour you have removed, the destroyed surface will take a wash, although not very well. Small areas of white, however, can be flicked out with a blade or painted on with Chinese white watercolour.

The granular effect here was achieved by blowing a wash of viridian with a hairdryer. When this was dry, I applied the dark green blobs, and then blew the wet paint through a straw. Some control over the general direction in which the paint goes is possible but this is a rather random technique.

This exercise shows how scratching can be used. Two simple flat washes were applied to the paper, and left to dry. A craft knife blade was scratched flatly over the water area to create the broken effect. The point of the blade was used to give the sharper white lines and the lighthouse.

Wax resist

When you draw with candle wax it doesn't completely cover the surface of the paper, particularly on a Rough or textured paper. Use a piece of ordinary white candle and rub it on to the parts you want to keep white. A subsequent wash cannot penetrate the wax but will lie in the crevices between, thereby giving a mottled broken effect. It is therefore unlike masking fluid, which will give you a clean, hard line (see pages 106-7). As the wax will stay on the paper you cannot change your mind and try to put a wash where the wax remains.

This technique is more suitable for larger, broader watercolours, because, although it can be controlled, it is only done so with difficulty. It is more usually used in a random or haphazard way; it does, however, produce interesting results on occasions.

Similar results can also be achieved with white wax crayons.

Above: Using wax as a resist repels a subsequent wash.

These poppies demonstrate how wax resist can be used. After sketching the design in pencil, I roughly drew in vertical lines using a piece of white candle. This acted as a wax resist and granulated the green wash which I laid over it. I then laid a light flat wash of raw sienna and cadmium red for the poppies. When this was completely dry, I again drew in a rather random way with my piece of candle to suggest the growth of the petals. This wax resist was overlaid with a wash of cadmium red mixed with a little cadmium yellow. Finally, the leaves were laid as a flat wash and parts of the flowers accentuated with darker streaks of red and purple.

Dabbing off and blotting

Apart from its use in removing colour, blotting paper is a real necessity for the watercolour artist. If you keep moistening an area of paint with water and blotting off you can almost eliminate a colour. Also, it is very useful to have a sheet of blotting paper on your work surface so that if you overcharge your brush you can lose some of the surplus by touching the blotting paper with your brush. In an emergency, such as a colour running or a drip of paint, blotting paper is indispensable.

Blotting paper removes areas of wet paint.

Blotting with crumpled tissue creates a texture.

Although you can use very absorbent tissue paper in the same way as blotting paper, it is more often used for creating texture. It gives a random effect, particularly useful in creating foliage. It is possible to use any absorbent material in this way – muslin, rags, string, or natural objects such as leaves. All of these can be either pressed into paint, placed on to the paper and rubbed on the back to create a texture, rather like using a stencil. Alternatively, place the dry material over wet paint on the paper to lift off areas of paint, thus creating a texture.

Scumbling

Although more widely used in oil painting, scumbling can also be useful to the watercolourist. Scumbling is really a dry-brush technique, used mainly for breaking one colour over another without obliterating the first. Many artists, including Eric Ravillious and Edward Bawden, have used it very successfully.

Load a brush with paint, keeping it fairly dry, and apply the pigment with a circular movement. It often helps if you pinch out the brush to splay

HOW TO SCUMBLE

Splay out the brush hairs and comb the colour on.

the hairs and virtually comb the colour on. Areas of white paper or a previous colour will show through. This effect does not work so well on a smooth-surfaced paper.

Similar effects can also be achieved by dragging the brush over the surface of the paper. For this the colour needs to be fairly dry. You can also achieve this dry-brush look by lifting the brush from the paper rapidly at the end of a stroke – the paint will leave a wispy dry-brush trail.

Lifting colour

Variations of this technique are used considerably by artists. Basically, when you have laid a wash of colour and while the paint is still wet, lift out the required area by wetting a large brush, squeezing it dry and mopping out the colour. The following are some common adaptations of this idea:

1 The edges of a wash can be softened by using a brush or sponge moistened in clean water and squeezed out to enable it to mop up surplus wet paint. This is illustrated on page 96.

2 If a wash has dried with a hard edge and it needs to be softened, wet inside the edge for about 6–12mm (¼–½in.), then, with a brush, work the paint in a circular motion until you can see the edge disappear. Blot off the water either with a squeezed-out brush or blotting paper.

3 If a colour has dried too dark and needs to be lightened, sponge over the whole surface with clean water and mop up with a squeezed-out sponge or brush. The harder you sponge, the more colour you will remove. This technique can be used over fairly large areas to lighten the colour a little overall. You will not, however, be able to get back to pure white paper because the watercolour will have left some stain.

4 Small areas and lines of paint can be lifted off with cottonwool buds (cotton swabs).

5 When the paint surface is completely dry you can lighten part or the whole of an area by using a soft eraser. However, if you rub too hard you will render the surface unusable for a further wash.

LIFTING TECHNIQUES

Use a cottonwool bud (swab) to blot small areas.

A brush can be used to mop out areas of wet paint.

A sponge is useful for lightening larger areas.

Masking fluid

Masking fluid is a liquid rubber solution which can be applied to areas of your painting where you don't want a wash to go. Its main value is that it will enable you to achieve clean crisp edges and, after it has been rubbed off, the surface can be painted over or left white. In this it differs from wax resist (see page 103). Masking fluid can be applied with an old watercolour brush, an oil hog-hair brush, a stippling brush, the edge of a piece of cardboard, a dip pen for lines and dots, or a ruling pen for long straight lines. Shake the bottle well. A word of warning: always clean your brush or pen in clean water immediately after use to remove the fluid completely.

The masking fluid can be applied to the white surface of the paper, or it can be used over an existing wash to preserve parts of that when you intend to paint another wash over the top. In both cases, the surface of the paper must be completely dry when you apply the fluid.

Right: In this instance, masking fluid was used to create a texture of tiny flowers in the foreground, and also on the frames of the greenhouse. After the masking fluid had been rubbed off, leaving white paper, watercolour was applied over some of these areas.

Left: The impact of the breaking wave in this illustration is created with masking fluid. I used masking fluid and a brush to draw in what would be the white of the breaking wave and dabbed on the white spots of the foreground. I then painted in the sky area and the water, creating the darker shadow under the wave, added wet into wet, and the foreground. When all the washes were dry, I rubbed off the masking fluid. At that stage I felt that there should be more white in the breaking wave, so I scratched a little of the colour away from the top of the wave.

USING MASKING FLUID

Paint with masking fluid those areas you wish to remain white.

When the fluid is dry, apply washes to the paper in the normal way – the unpainted surface will be protected.

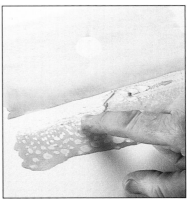

When the washes are completely dry, rub off the mask. Make sure your finger is clean!

Project: Painting a landscape

For this project, I decided to use an existing drawing that was made 'on the spot' as a basis from which to paint. The original was drawn in charcoal and pencil without any colour. This was backed up at the time with a sketch and colour notes. This

demonstration offers the chance of using many of the techniques outlined so far. Don't try to copy it exactly – it is important to select a subject that interests you and one that you feel confident enough to tackle – but try to pick a subject that will give you the opportunity to try out as many techniques as possible. Finally, don't worry if this doesn't turn out to be a masterpiece. As an artist, these are early days for you: the

You will need
- ☐ a drawing board with stretched paper
- ☐ two jars of clean water
- ☐ paints
- ☐ brushes
- ☐ a white plate or palette
- ☐ a stick of charcoal
- ☐ a soft pencil and eraser
- ☐ natural sponges
- ☐ masking fluid
- ☐ razor or craft knife blades
- ☐ a toothbrush
- ☐ a ruler
- ☐ drinking straws
- ☐ a piece of cardboard

The notes on colour (above) and original 'on the spot' drawing.

important thing at this stage is that you enjoy your painting. The paper selected for this project was Arches 140lb (295gsm) and I stretched two ½ Imperial sheets as described on page 78. It is always worth having a spare sheet of paper ready stretched when you start on a project. If you do find that you want to start again, it is very annoying to have to wait several hours for a newly stretched sheet to dry naturally. The size of the painting here is 300 × 430mm (13 × 17in.) so there will be a margin inside the gumstrip.

An initial wash of raw sienna over most of the painting.

Sponging in the areas of grass.

The initial stippling on the trees.

Preliminary sketches

To start with, I lightly sketched the main lines of the composition on the stretched paper in charcoal; this enabled me to correct the drawing or composition easily with an eraser. After I was satisfied, I dusted off the charcoal with a rag, then established the drawing more carefully in pencil. Treat the paper with care – don't draw too heavily or rub out too vigorously and use a fairly soft pencil, such as a 2B.

The first washes

I then laid a flat wash of raw sienna over the whole composition, except for the sky and the water. This was done to help unify the subsequent colours and to give an overall warm glow to the painting. If there are a few islands of white left, however, it will give more variety to the colours you use in overpainting.

Don't be fussy about the painting's edges; run the colour beyond the limit of your composition – the mount (mat) will cover this anyway.

The sky area was put in next. I first sponged over it with clean water, then prepared the three washes on separate palettes. I started at the top with a wash of cobalt blue. This was allowed to run down for about half the sky area, then, while this was still wet, one horizontal brush stroke of cadmium yellow was flooded into it and allowed to run down. While this was still wet the mauve colour was put in with two horizontal strokes. This produces the variegated wet-into-wet wash. I mopped up the excess wash that had accumulated at the bottom with a squeezed-out brush, then allowed this to dry.

The broad details

The grass was a mixture of viridian and cadmium yellow, applied with a large size sponge. Painting leaves or grass in detail is tedious. An open-textured sponge creates a texture which parallels that of grass and leaves more easily. I gave some areas a second dab of colour after the first was dry for added depth. When all this was dry, I put a few

The range of tones from light to dark is established at this early stage.

strokes of paint on to the staging. I then started to stipple in the trees with a mixture of prussian blue and raw sienna. This helped me to establish the range of tones, from light to dark, at a fairly early stage of the painting.

Adding texture

I used masking fluid on the path, and applied it with a brush in blobs. After allowing it to dry, I put a wash of indigo and alizarin crimson over the path area with some raw sienna run into the foreground. When all this was dry, the masking fluid was rubbed off. The texture resembling stones was created by putting a few darker blobs of colour over the top of this whole area.

I used masking fluid on the path.

Maintaining unity

Normally in a painting it helps to keep the unity if you work over the whole surface and don't finish off one part at a time. For this reason, I added more interest to the foreground by applying some splatter and scratching areas away. I then intensified the stippling on the trees to make it darker, and added more colour and texture to the grass. I also did some more work on the staging, including painting an area of cadmium red on one of the boats. This ensured that the staging area did not fall behind the rest of the painting. The distance was added in grey and some brush strokes of pale cobalt blue in the water.

Scratching here is used to create a flat plane.

The darker details

At this stage, I did some preliminary work on the masts. I painted the edge of a piece of cardboard and used this as a template for them.

Although my original 'on-the-spot' drawing did not have the bush in the foreground I decided to add it to the painting. I find it often helps to have something fairly large and dark in the foreground to make the distance lie back. The bush was made by mixing a dark wash of burnt umber, putting a few wet blobs at the bottom edge, then blowing it with a drinking straw; the leaves are the natural shape of brush strokes applied very freshly and allowed to dry.

The principal areas of texture completed.

Unifying the composition

Towards the completion of a painting, it is helpful to stand back and assess what needs to be done additionally to unify the composition. At this stage, I was able to see what the final effect of the painting was going to be, and decide how I should finish it.

I decided that the focal point of the staging and the boats still needed quite a lot of attention. The focal point of a painting is often finished to a higher degree than the rest of the composition but it is difficult to ascertain exactly what needs to be done until the rest of the painting is finished. The staging needed to be painted crisply since to a

Preliminary work on the masts.

Blowing through a straw to indicate branches.

certain extent the success or failure of the finished watercolour depended on it.

The contrast of the dark staging and the feeling of light, particularly on the water, is one of the major factors in the success of the painting and one of my main reasons for selecting this subject. I enhanced the feeling of light by increasing the contrast between the banks and the water, and between the water and the masts and rigging of the boats. I painted these details with a fine brush to ensure that they had the crispness and freshness that I wanted to achieve. To finish off, I added a few darker touches here and there to give sparkle.

The darker touches, painted last, add contrast and sparkle to the painting.

113

Subjects for the watercolourist

Almost any subject is suitable for making a watercolour – the success of a painting depends on your vision as an artist and your ability to express your feelings. It is through these feelings, expressed in a visual form, that you can help others to see and appreciate the world about them in a new way.

Painting familiar things like your garden or the view from your window, even your pet (top), has many advantages.

Flower studies make interesting paintings.

Choosing your subject

It is important in selecting your subject to see things freshly and in terms of painting – that is, in terms of tones, colours, textures and lines, rather than objectively or figuratively.

There is no need to go miles from home in order to find a subject to paint; in fact, you will probably produce a more successful painting if the subject is something you know intimately, in your own home or garden, or an area of the countryside you know well and love. Until you have had more experience, it is not advisable to try to paint the figure, particularly nude, in watercolour. Flesh tones are more difficult to achieve in watercolour than, say, in oils. There is the added problem of trying to paint a subject that moves about, and you will have enough problems without worrying about a model who will not stay still. This also applies if you'd like to paint your pets – choose a time when they are asleep!

It is not always possible to sit down with your watercolour kit and paint just when you feel like it, but if you carry a sketchbook around with you you can always make a note of something that interests you. This is also a good way of improving your drawing. Buy a sketchbook that will fit into your pocket or bag and whenever you have a spare moment draw whatever you can see – a pair of shoes, a line of washing, the kitchen sink, the breakfast table, an apple, and so on. Drawing is fundamental to art and it needs to be practised constantly. It does need discipline, however, to enable you to develop the necessary hand–eye co-ordination.

While you are still familiarizing yourself with the medium, don't always work on the same size paper – if you are close to what you intend to paint, try working on a larger scale. Whatever your subject and size of painting, you will need something in the composition that you can use to measure scale; in a still life it could be a particular pot, it may be a tree in a landscape, or just the length of a particular line. This then becomes your module and everything is related to it in scale.

When you are selecting objects to paint, don't worry too much about arranging them: a good painting can be made from a completely haphazard group of items or indeed from something in itself quite insignificant.

Portraits, full or head and shoulders, though difficult, are worth trying.

The choice of subject for still lifes is endless – items in themselves insignificant can make interesting compositions.

Finally, although being an artist is fascinating, fulfilling and rewarding, remember that you will always be learning. The more you know, the less you seem to know. But, like anything worth while, you must work at it to reap the rewards. You cannot, therefore, learn to paint simply by reading about it. You must produce lots of paintings to become familiar with what you can (and can't) do. If you develop a love of the medium, and a desire to paint, all the effort and possible disappointments will seem unimportant.

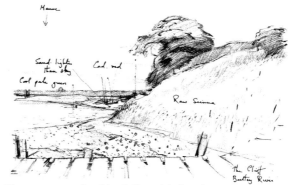

Always carry a sketchbook for quick drawings.

116

Approaches to watercolour

The paintings on these pages are a selection of historical and contemporary works by artists in watercolour. They show different treatments and different subjects and emphasize that there is no one way to approach a subject – there are as many ways as there are artists. Similarly, there is no one way to use watercolour paint. Andrew Wyeth, Hans Schwarz, Olwen Jones and I use watercolour transparently (this is known as the 'English' method), but Samuel Palmer and Christa Gaa in their works have used gouache (or body colour) – which is not transparent – mixed with the transparent watercolour.

I hope that these examples will demonstrate that watercolour is by no means a precious isolated medium, it is another way of expressing yourself. Most artists are not solely watercolourists or oil painters or draughtsmen they use whichever medium they feel best expresses their ideas at any particular time.

Samuel Palmer 'In a Shoreham Garden' 275 × 218mm (11 × 8¼in.). This example shows how the combination of transparent watercolour with gouache and pen lends itself to a decorative and textural approach. The gouache is used most thickly in the lighter areas.

Christa Gaa 'Still Life with Nepalese Bird' 192 × 216mm (8 × 9in.). This watercolour looks deceptively simple, but the quality of light, composition and colour are carefully considered. The combination of watercolour and gouache expresses the feeling of intense overhead light and atmosphere. The losing and finding of the tones and edge qualities also contribute to making this a very lovely painting.

Andrew Wyeth 'Southern Comfort' 563 × 750mm (21¾ × 30in.). This watercolour was painted in 1987 and is typical of the work of Andrew Wyeth. Obviously, the painting has a strong illustrational content yet it is so much more. The very strong composition and limited use of colour, and the artist's understanding and care over edge qualities, give this painting a great sense of poetry. The texture of the paint surface, the transparent use of watercolour and the use of dry brushwork typify his work.

Hans Schwarz 'Kitchen Jars and Bottles on a White Table' 500 × 675mm (20 × 27in.). 'I have only a white piece of paper and a few tubes of watercolour to represent this complex arrangement of jars and bottles. Faithful representation is less important to me than a rich colour pattern and a lively flow of paint. Green becomes the predominant colour. From the left background it threads its way to the jars on the right. Red, blue, orange, violet and yellow interrupt the green, bringing forward and defining the objects in space. Juxtaposed complementary colours – red and green, violet and yellow, give recession and sparkle.'

Olwen Jones 'Winter Geraniums' 600 × 475mm (24 × 19in.). 'This watercolour was painted with an afternoon light in my greenhouse. It depicts geranium cuttings overwintering, looking rather sad among the netting used for diffusing light and several odd panes of glass. The light and reflections from the panes were what first attracted me to the subject. The whole composition had a transparent quality with plenty of texture, which I always use a lot in my paintings. I also liked the contrast between the soft shapes of the geraniums and foliage, and the sharp hard edges of the glass. Reflections, whether in glass or a mirror, give an added dimension to a composition; you are never quite sure whether an image is real or reflected. In this painting I used only transparent watercolour and some masking fluid.'

Charles Bartlett 'Lakeside' 437 × 575mm (17½ × 23in.). 'This watercolour was painted in the studio from drawings and notes made on the spot. By working in this way I am able to consider and organize my composition. The feeling I got for the subject was the poetry of place, of tranquillity and stillness and a soft feeling of light on the reeds and in the water. It is not essential in watercolour to use a broken "washy" technique always. The dark silhouette of the distant trees accentuated the light shining on the feathery heads of the reeds. I used masking fluid fairly extensively on the reeds.'

119

Project: Still life

Art is about expressing oneself and not just copying what happens to be in front of you; it is about ideas and feelings. Above all, it is to be enjoyed. Once you have mastered the basic techniques of watercolour painting, expressing emotion through creating a feeling of light, freshness, sparkle and texture, for example, becomes more important than an accurate representation of what you see in front of you. This is what I try to achieve in my painting. This project interested me for a number of reasons. Probably the most important is the quality of light – I painted against the light on a windowsill in my studio – but I was also attracted by the colour and variety of textures, the light showing through the lace curtains and the stripes on the cloth, which also introduce perspective (the vanishing point is the centre of vision). The purple stripes are a complementary colour to the green of the landscape and apples. This subject also demonstrates the importance of choosing an appropriate eye-level. I selected a high eye-level so that I would be looking down on the striped cloth and into the basket, and also enough of the landscape over the windowsill to give a different dimension to the picture. This watercolour is painted on T.H. Saunders 140lb (295gsm) paper which I had stretched, and the image size is 380 × 310mm (16 × 13in.).

You will need
☐ a drawing board with stretched paper
☐ two jars of clean water
☐ paints
☐ brushes
☐ a white plate or palette
☐ a sponge
☐ a toothbrush
☐ a knife
☐ masking tape

Initial stages

The composition of this watercolour was decided after I had made several preliminary sketches. The drawing was first laid in with charcoal which was then dusted down, and the image was drawn in in pencil. Although the drawing is fairly accurate, I didn't want to labour it as I intended to keep the watercolour free. If you are over-careful with the drawing there is a tendency to fill in the shapes with paint in local areas, and this can produce a very stilted picture.

The sky was painted wet into wet, starting with cobalt blue, grading to pale raw sienna and then purple. The green (a mix of cadmium yellow and cobalt blue) was laid in as a flat wash. Raw sienna was loosely painted on parts of the basket and the foreground, and while this was still wet burnt sienna was flooded into the foreground.

The palest washes were put in first.

The trees were added over the flat wash of the landscape, then a paler wash of thin light prussian blue and a little burnt sienna was carried over the lace curtains and blotted off with blotting paper. The frames of the windows were added after the landscape was dry. I used burnt sienna, indigo and crimson lake for this wash. The apple and the shadow from the vase and plate were also indicated at this stage.

First details

I decided to finish the flowers and vase completely at this stage. Normally I like to keep the whole painting going but flowers move and die, so although the drawing of the flowers was fairly detailed, I painted them broadly to try to keep the feeling of light. The colours I used on the flowers were cadmium yellow, burnt sienna and purple (mixed from prussian blue and alizarin crimson). The cut glass vase was painted using cadmium yellow and cobalt blue, keeping the edges and contrasts sharp. I then lightly indicated the plate and knife.

Creating the flat planes

At this stage, I was anxious to establish the flat plane of the table and create a feeling of space. I felt that the stripes on the tablecloth would achieve this so I decided to tackle them next. Once they were done, I could see that they had achieved the perspective and plane of the table top.

The painting was now beginning to take shape and it was easier to appreciate what was needed next. I decided I could not delay work on the curtain and basket as these would establish if the painting was going to be successful or not.

The background completed.

The flowers nearly completed.

Painting the purple striped tablecloth.

The tablecloth establishes the plane of the table top.

Adding warmth

The pattern on the lace curtain was painted using masking fluid. I tried to consider the counter-change brought about by the holes in the lace being seen against the sky and landscape. I put a warm pale wash over the curtain (once the masking fluid was dry), and when the wash was dry, rubbed off the mask. I now felt that the purple stripes made the table top too cold so I added some broken raw sienna to the lace mat.

Creating light

To help establish the overall feeling of light in the painting the dark note of the basket was added next; this was important as it balanced the composition. I painted it in warm dark tones (burnt umber and burnt sienna) to help bring it forward from the landscape and background.

The curtain was painted with a wash of raw sienna.

The basket is the darkest note of the painting.

As I was painting against the light, the basket cast a deep shadow and I put this in next as it helped to make the basket 'sit down' on the plane of the table.

The basket's shadow makes it 'sit down' on the table.

Covering the paper surface

In any painting before you can really begin to see the final result it is necessary to get all the white paper covered. The fruit in the basket was the last unpainted area and so I tackled this next. I was careful to retain a light top edge to the basket since it would help to convey a feeling of light. The shadow from the window frame falling on the cloth was put in with a simple wash of cobalt blue – blue is a colour that will lie back in a painting.

The finishing touches

At this stage, the painting was nearly finished; the surface was all covered and I felt the unity of the composition was coming together. I could now see what was needed to finish the painting – the curtain was not dark enough, the flowers and vase needed some strengthening, the foreground wasn't dark enough, and the lace table mat required work. These final touches are vital in any composition, they often bring the painting to life. At this stage, you may want to link the dark areas together, or to emphasize a particular movement.

The lace on the table mat was suggested rather delicately so as not to lose the overall feeling of whiteness and so I used a very fine brush. The outline shape was created by the dark stripes of the cloth; I felt it would be more satisfactory painted in this way as in this kind of painting outlining the shapes themselves may flatten the composition. Also I did not want to lose the feeling of light and the delicacy of the painting – where the far edge of the plate melts into the lace mat, for example.

The darker details

It now seemed to me that the landscape and background were too light for the weight of colour in the foreground. I decided to darken the curtain and also fill in the light hole behind the

Covering the final areas of white paper.

basket. Having done that, I felt that the flowers didn't seem to take their correct place in space because they were so pale, and so I darkened under their front edges. This pulled them forward, and linked the dark of the basket to the dark horizontal frame of the window. I did some scratching on the curtain and on the tablecloth to give small flecks of white which you often get when you are looking into strong light. This also helped the basket's shadow 'lie down'. Finally, I painted the foreground vigorously in a dark warm colour to pull the table edge forward.

When you finish a painting and stand back to look at it, you will probably always feel that some parts are more successful than others. Do try to restrain yourself from starting to niggle at these areas – this is the easiest way to destroy the feeling of freshness and light you have achieved.

The lace is suggested delicately.

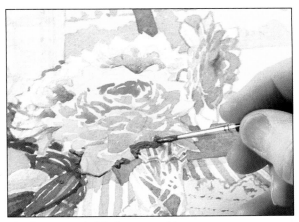

The flowers needed darkening at this stage.

The painting is nearly finished at this stage.

The warm foreground pulls the table edge forward.

PART THREE

Starting in Oils

Introduction

Oil painting is one of the oldest and most widely used methods of painting, and because of the number of examples reproduced in books and on display in public art galleries, it has become the most familiar way of painting to us. This is probably one of the initial reasons why many people who wish to take up painting choose to work in oils. However once this decision has been made, one quickly realizes that there are many good reasons why the medium has survived for so long – oil has been widely used since the fifteenth century – and retained its popularity in the face of such modern alternatives as acrylics and resin-based paints.

'Frosted Grass' 500 × 600mm (20 × 24in.). This picture shows how the palette knife can be used as an expressive way of making marks which relate to the subject matter, in this case frosty grass. By using the edge of the knife I was able to give that sharp, crisp quality needed to convey the feeling and surface texture of frost on the rather linear shapes of the grass.

Oil paint is pigment that has been ground in an oil-based medium, usually 'linseed'. The actual pigment is often the same one that is used in watercolour or gouache (body colour or poster paint); it is the preparation that gives it certain unique qualities not present in other paints. Firstly, it tends to impart a richer feeling to the colour. It also makes it a very flexible medium, allowing it to be used in a variety of ways ranging from very thick (called 'impasto') to thin paint which is almost the consistency of watercolour. This also means that the application of oil paint has endless possibilities. It can be applied in almost any way one wishes – by brush, knives, rags and even fingers. There are also notable examples of the paint having been thrown on to the surface.

Although the beginner may feel somewhat intimidated by the long history of oil painting and the high degree of technical craftsmanship of most of the more familiar pictures, due to its flexibility oil paint is, in fact, an ideal medium for the beginner.

J.M.W. Turner 'Norham Castle' 908 × 1219mm (33¾ × 48in.). This beautiful example of painting shows thin transparent paint throughout the whole picture. It has the quality of watercolour which gives the light translucence to the subject. The few impasto areas of paint are reserved for accents of light, catching clouds or water and act as a complement to the thin paint, and give a sparkle within the hazy sunlit atmosphere.

Martin Baldwin 'Portrait of a French Girl' 860 × 610mm (33 × 24in.). In this portrait the artist's careful build up using thin paint on a precise drawing base allows him to explore in detail the smaller forms of the head and drapery. Once the large areas had been broadly laid in, the artist used smaller and finer brushes such as sables for the fine detail. It is a painting which shows that the artist derives obvious pleasure in the pursuit of close observation and carefully modelled forms. Although this example is a portrait, the same approach can be used in any form of painting such as landscape, still life, or even abstract work.

One advantage that it has over most other paints is its drying time, which is considerably longer than water- or acrylic-based paints. This means that one can put the paint on to the canvas, then scrape it off, and work and rework areas of the painting over a much longer period of time.

Oil painting can have a certain air of mystery about it when you come to it as a total beginner, even though you may have worked with other mediums. There is no real reason why this should be so. By applying a practical and logical step-by-step approach to the subject, I will show that anyone who is interested enough to want to try can develop the skills and techniques through which to enhance their natural creativity and enjoy the fresh experience that can be gained by working with oil paints.

The great age of oil painting from which many of the most familiar examples date is probably the Renaissance, although there are also notable Impressionist and Modern paintings. This goes some way to supporting the idea that if the rules are adhered to, the other great quality that oil paint possesses is durability. There are many paintings now hundreds of years old that still retain the freshness of a new work. Sadly there are also many that are in a bad state of decay and preservation due either to neglect or to bad craftsmanship and materials.

There are some good examples of the use of oil techniques set out in these pages, but the most inspirational experience to be had is to go out and look at the real thing. They do not necessarily have to be works by great masters, and while looking at paintings in books can and does whet the appetite, this cannot be compared with the direct experience. No matter how good the reproduction is, you can never really experience fully the textural aspects of the brush or knife marks or the translucent qualities of the paint. By looking at paintings in galleries or museums and seeing and trying to understand how the artist actually executed them, not only will you give yourself hours of enjoyment, but you will also learn a great deal about oil-painting technique.

'Sleeping Dog' 900 × 1200mm (36 × 48in.). This painting gives a feeling of the gestural quality that painting can have. The large format allows the artist to make broad bold marks with large brushes. It is a painting which combines many aspects of applying paint; some has been painted wet into wet, while other areas have brush marks dragged across thick dry paint. The paint has been built up in this way throughout and gives the picture a richness of surface and colour.

Materials and equipment

The wide range of materials available to the oil painter, most of which are manufactured to a high standard, can be a source of difficulty and confusion for the beginner: where to start? what to choose? how much to spend? In this section, the various materials available and how to use them is outlined and clarified. This will enable you to make choices based on your knowledge of the products and, as you become more experienced, your own personal needs.

Oil colours: (clockwise from bottom left) flake white, cobalt blue, cadmium yellow, cadmium red, viridian, burnt sienna, raw umber, alizarin crimson, burnt umber – all Artists' colours; yellow ochre, terre verte and raw sienna – Students' colours.

Oil paints

Oil paints are produced in two qualities – Artists' colour and Students' colour. Artists' colour is very much more expensive, due to the origin of the pigments themselves: the very best are used in Artists' colours. You will also notice that there is a price variation within the range of colour; this is because of the rarity of some of the pigments, which affects the cost of manufacture. The texture of the paint is also generally smoother, although this is hardly noticeable to the beginner and does not significantly affect the look of the painting.

Tubes of Artists' colour usually have a coding denoting the price range of the particular colour.

Students' colour is manufactured using synthetic dyes and inexpensive pigments as substitutes for the rarer more expensive ones. The texture of these paints is also coarser as the pigments are not as finely ground. Although the Students' range is much cheaper than the Artists' range, there are some colours which are not normally available in it (such as the cadmium colours, cobalt blue and green, and vermilion) because of costs. If you compare Artists' colours with the Students' range you will notice a marked difference in strength and brightness, particularly when mixed with white; Artists' colour will need less to maintain the density of colour.

When you start painting, you will notice that certain colours take longer to dry than others: earth colours dry fairly quickly, while some reds

can take three or four days. The earth colours are: yellow ochre, red ochre, raw umber, burnt umber, terre verte, raw sienna and burnt sienna.

With the exception of white (which can be purchased in a large tube), tubes of colour are produced in two sizes. The 37ml (1¼oz./No. 14) size is the most practical for the majority of colours, but because one tends to use far more white than any other colour it is advisable to buy white in the larger (56ml/2oz./No. 20) size. Students' quality paints are also available in 200ml (8oz.) size tins, which unless used fairly quickly will skin over and dry out. They also tend to contain more oil than the tube equivalent.

Having described the basic differences between the two qualities of paint, I think that for the beginner Students' colours are perfectly adequate (to start with). The last thing you want is to feel inhibited by the cost and wastage of your materials, and, at this stage, the difference in results will not be noticeable. However as you progress and gain confidence you can increase your range by adding Artists' colours, as the two types of paint mix perfectly well together. This will also help to keep your initial costs down.

Paintboxes

There are many pre-selected paintboxes on the market. Some of the more expensive ones are beautifully made and can be rather seductive to the beginner. Their big disadvantage, however, is that the selection of colours has been put together by someone else. I think it is important for beginners to make their own selection based on their personal needs and development, and at a realistic cost. Eventually most artists need a container of some sort for all their painting paraphernalia, especially if they paint out of doors. When that time comes the decision will be one of personal preference. You may choose to buy a purpose-made paintbox and supply the materials yourself, or find a convenient-sized plastic or wooden box, or a stout canvas bag to hold all your equipment.

Brushes

There are several types and qualities of brush on the market for the painter to choose from. The most popular brushes for oil painting are bristle made from bleached hog's-hair, and soft brushes made from sable hair. Hog's-hair bristle brushes are fairly stiff, hold the paint well and are manufactured in three different shapes:

Flat brushes have a square-ended shape that is good for applying dabs of colour. If you use the edge, it will give a nice sharp linear mark, useful for drawing.

Round brushes in the larger sizes are good for covering large areas; smaller ones are ideal for initial drawing in.

Filberts are a cross between a flat and a round, except that the shape tapers to a point.

Sable brushes are usually used for detailed work or for thin fine glazes, and they are also ideal for the first drawing in. Some artists prefer to execute a whole painting with this type of brush. These brushes are extremely expensive and unless looked after carefully, they will deteriorate in a very short time. These brushes are not really suited to a rough surface or ground, and will soon show signs of wear if used on one – the hairs tend to become brittle and break off and the brush soon loses its shape.

Synthetic bristle and hair brushes, usually made from nylon, are now also available. They come in the same shapes as the hog's-hair and sable types but are considerably cheaper and for the most part, are very good and hard-wearing. When choosing your brushes it is very much a personal preference, rather in the way that you build up your range of colours. Some artists will use a great many brushes, others will paint with just a few. As a beginner you really need to try various shapes and sizes to enable you to decide what suits your way of working. You may even find that you prefer the synthetic fibre brushes to the more traditional bristle.

The size of the brush is indicated by a number on the handle; the same size numbers do not apply to both hog's-hair and sable brushes, however, so a No. 1 bristle will not be the same actual size as No. 1 in a sable.

Whereas with paints, you can get away with mixing Students' and Artists' colours, I think that brushes should always be of the best quality from the start. If looked after properly they will last for years and keep their shape.

Brush care

Caring for your brush is of the utmost importance, not only to your pocket but to the quality of your painting. Brushes should be thoroughly cleaned at the end of each day's painting. Wipe the excess oil paint off with a rag or tissue and then rinse with turpentine (white spirit/paint thinner will do for this) until you feel that it is as clean as you can get it. Finally, wash with soap and water by rubbing the brush on to an ordinary household bar of soap and then working up a lather in the palm of your hand. Repeat until the soap suds show no sign of colour and then rinse with warm water. If you shape the brush while it is still wet, when it dries you will find it has kept its shape.

Palette knives

Palette knives have two main functions: applying the paint to the picture surface and scraping it off. It is possible to paint either a part or the whole of the picture with a knife if you desire a rich, textured surface. It is essential for scraping areas of paint from the picture surface to enable them to be reworked if necessary. Its use also extends to mixing colour and cleaning the palette. A wide range of shapes and sizes is available, the choice you make is again (rather like your brushes) a matter of preference. However, you certainly would not need more than one to start with. The most practical type for the beginner is the trowel shape or painting knife, recognizable by its cranked handle and more flexible blade.

Brushes: (left to right) hog's-hair flats, rounds and filberts of varying widths, large sable wash brush, sable flats and rounds of different sizes.

Right: Palette knives are available in various sizes and shapes – a trowel shape is probably the most practical for a beginner.

Palettes

The first thing to remember about a palette is that it is only the surface on which you set out and mix your paints. There is a wide variety of shapes and sizes available to the artist: you will need to decide at the outset whether you wish to hold the palette or rest it on the table or on some other convenient flat surface.

Most palettes are made to be held, and have a hole for the thumb. They come in two main shapes: kidney shape, sometimes called a studio palette, and rectangular shape. Rectangular ones are usually smaller and will fit into a paintbox. More expensive ones are usually made from mahogany but there are many made from other woods, from plastic or even from paper.

It is not essential to have either of the traditional shapes as long as you have a clean smooth surface. As you will find for most of your basic materials, there are cheap alternatives: a piece of hardboard (Masonite), plywood or perspex (plastic) will suit just as well as long as you seal the surface. The traditional way of doing this is to rub linseed oil into the wood and repeat the process over two or three days. This will prevent the surface soaking up the oil from the paint. However, a quicker way to seal the surface is to use shellac or button polish, either of which can be painted on, or rubbed in. Paper palettes are very practical when you are in a hurry; by simply tearing off the top layer of paper and disposing of it, you are left with a clean white surface for next time.

Diluents

As well as being used to clean your palette and brushes, the function of diluents is to thin or dilute the paint and help it spread over the painting surface.

It is essential that the solvent used should evaporate from the paint as it dries. Turpentine is the best solvent and there are two types: distilled turpentine (the more expensive) is pure turpentine made from pine resin and gives off a strong and distinctive although not unpleasant smell; turpentine substitute (or white spirit) is made from petroleum oils. Both can be used safely to thin paint but pure turpentine is best for painting, and white spirit is best kept for cleaning purposes.

It is worth pointing out that both sorts of turpentine have a strong smell and that some people are either allergic to turpentine products or just cannot stand the smell. To overcome this, manufacturers Pelican introduced Master Colour, a paint which has all the properties of oil paint, but it is soluble in water and is completely odourless. At present, the colour range is rather more limited than the traditional oil paints.

Mediums

The subject of mediums is a complex one for beginners. To start with, quite a number are produced. Some are very traditional mediums and binders of oil and varnishes of varying recipes, others are more modern acrylics and resins, produced by various manufacturers. Like diluents, mediums can be used to thin the paint, but they are also used to modify the paint in some way – perhaps to improve its consistency for impasto painting or to increase its drying time. Linseed oil has been the most popular medium through the ages, but other oils such as poppy are also used. However, I feel that the standard of paint manufacture today is of such a high level and consistency that unless you need a specific quality – a very glossy paint, for example, or an absence of brush marks – as a beginner, you need not concern yourself with the problem of what to use at this point. Later you can experiment with different kinds – nearly all the bottles have labels which explain the different attributes of the particular mediums. For example, pure linseed oil slows drying, and increases the gloss of the paint; poppy oil gives the paint a creamy consistency, good for *alla prima* – the method of oil painting used for the projects in this section; Wingel is good for glazing and thicker paint; and Liquin is good for glazing, gives gloss and increases the drying time.

A dipper (palette cup) is simply a receptacle for the painting medium and cleaning agent. They are usually made of metal, can be clipped on to the palette, and are especially useful if you are painting outdoors. For cleaning brushes, have a jar or old tin for the cleaning agent.

Easels

There are several types of easel available to the artist: the main point to remember is that the purpose of the easel is to provide a firm and stable support to your picture while you are working, so make sure that you pick the right one for the job. The most versatile is the radial or studio easel, which are manufactured by most of the well-known art suppliers. All are made to a similar pattern, and although fairly expensive will last a lifetime. They will support your smallest picture to a work about 1.75m (6ft) high comfortably.

A light sketching easel is ideal for outside work. These are folding and can be easily carried, but obviously the size of picture they can support is limited. Sketching easels are made in either wood or metal: the metal ones are lighter but slightly more expensive.

The table easel is a useful way of supporting a painting, especially if you are working in an area with limited floor space.

In the absence of an easel it is possible to use the back of an old chair as a support for a small painting.

You may find some or all of these items useful in your work. An easel provides a firm support for your paintings, and a palette and dippers of some kind are necessary. You will also need a diluent although you will probably not need to worry about mediums at this stage.

Painting supports

The painting support is the surface on to which you apply your paint. For oil painting, this has to be a non-porous surface and have sufficient tooth to hold the paint. To achieve this the surface of most supports has to be sealed. The most traditional material for painting is canvas which has been in use as a support since the fifteenth century. As well as its pleasing natural qualities of weave and texture, it has the advantage of being light and easy to carry. There are several different textures or weights of canvas available and what you decide on really does depend on the way you

Oil painting supports: (from left) smooth cartridge paper, rough cartridge paper, canvas board, Daler board, unprimed canvas, primed canvas, ready stretched canvas, strengthened hardboard and muslin.

prefer to work. If you paint thinly and with a great deal of detail, then you will find that a smooth-grain canvas will suit you best. On the other hand, a heavier coarse grain will be better for the thicker impasto way of working. All art suppliers sell ready prepared canvases in a variety of shapes and sizes but you will find that they are expensive. A much cheaper way of working with canvas is to buy the canvas by the metre or yard and stretch and prepare it yourself. Stretching the canvas is not difficult. The wooden stretcher pieces you will need are available either at the art suppliers or canvas stockists.

When you buy your canvas you will find that you have a wide choice. The best quality and therefore most expensive is linen canvas, easily recognizable by its darker brown colour. A cheaper version is cotton canvas which is also available in various textures and weights and is generally the most popular. You will notice that it is also much whiter than linen canvas.

Priming a canvas

Having stretched it, you are ready to prime the canvas. The purpose of priming is to separate the painting from the canvas – if the paint is applied to the raw canvas it will soak into the fibres of the material and eventually rot them. It will also have an effect on the look of the painting: paint used in this way has a dull, rather dry look. There are many examples of modern paintings which have been carried out in this way because this quality has been deliberately looked for, and the artist has stained the raw canvas. This will no doubt pose some interesting problems for future picture restorers and conservationists.

Sealing the surface is the first task, this is done with glue size (coating). Rabbit skin size is the finest and tends to be more flexible than other sizes, but really most commercial glue size will do the job. Two coats should be applied to the canvas, the first of which should be well brushed in; ideally a day should be left between each coat.

STRETCHING A CANVAS

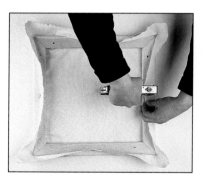

1 Lay the stretcher frame on a flat surface on top of the canvas. Mark off the amount of canvas you require, allowing a minimum of 5cm (2in.) overlap on all four sides. Remove the stretcher and cut the canvas parallel to the weave. Replace the stretcher on top of the canvas, making sure all the angles of the frame are square.

2 Starting on one side, fold the canvas over the stretcher and tack it with a staple gun in the centre. Pull the canvas taut and repeat this on the opposite side, then do the two remaining sides. Continue round the stretcher in this way, always working on opposite sides, and from the centre to the corners.

3 When you come to the corners, pull the corner of the canvas over, keeping it taut.

The next stage is to apply the ground. This will be the surface for your painting and will also serve as a further protection for the support. The ground should be an oil-based one which when dry should remain flexible to prevent the surface from cracking. There are many ready prepared grounds which can be purchased in artists' materials shops. They are always white, and at least two coats should be applied, but again this will depend on personal preferences as to the quality of surface you wish to achieve.

Another, quicker, method of preparing the canvas is to use acrylic primer which is water based and should be applied directly to the canvas without the glue size. This requires three or four coats, the first of which should be thinner and thoroughly brushed into the canvas. Priming in this way results in a good flexible ground which will take oil paint or acrylic paints equally well.

It is also possible to buy newly primed canvas by the metre or yard; this is fairly expensive but is still a good deal cheaper than buying ready stretched canvases.

The most commonly used support apart from canvas is hardboard (Masonite). This is a much cheaper alternative and has the advantage of strength – it will take more knocks than canvas. It is, however, far heavier and a larger size will need wooden supports to prevent it bending and warping. Hardboard still has to be sealed and given a ground in the same way as canvas. The most popular method is to use acrylic primer or plain white emulsion (latex) paint which eliminates the need for glue size and is cheaper by far. The finished surface is, obviously, hard and smooth, unlike canvas.

Never use the rough side of the hardboard to paint on, for although it superficially has the appearance of canvas, it is entirely unsuitable, due to its unsympathetic mechanical surface. It is almost impossible to get rid of paint if you do paint on it. If you do want a canvas type of

4 Fold one section of the canvas neatly into the frame, then fold the other section over it.

5 Staple through all the layers. It is important not to pull the canvas too tight, it should be taut and smooth. If it is too tight when you prime it the shrinkage caused by the priming will warp the shape and if really tight can split the canvas.

6 When you purchased your stretcher pieces you should have been given eight little wedges, two for each corner. These should be gently pushed into the slots on the inside of the corners. They enable you to tighten the canvas if it should slacken off due to atmospheric changes in the course of painting.

COVERING HARDBOARD

1 Cut a piece of muslin approximately 5cm (2in.) larger all round than the piece of hardboard you intend to use.

2 Glue the muslin to the shiny side of the hardboard with acrylic or emulsion primer. Brush through the fabric.

3 Turn the board over and glue the muslin to the hardboard supports. Make sure you glue well into the corners.

surface, muslin can be attached to the hardboard. Use the acrylic or emulsion primer to glue the muslin to the hardboard, making sure that you leave enough material (about 5cm/2in.) to turn over round the edges. This will need several coats of priming but will produce an interesting surface at low cost.

There are other ready prepared supports available in the form of oil painting papers, some bound like sketchbooks, and canvas boards or Daler boards which have a canvas-like surface. These are fairly inexpensive, and readily available. Lastly, plain heavy cartridge (drawing) paper and card can be used for oil painting if you treat the surface with emulsion paint before you start. This will provide a good working surface for quick sketches out of doors or in the studio.

This is an example of oil paint used on cartridge (drawing) paper. It was a quick study, and the paint was kept thin, almost like a wash of watercolour except that, by using oil paint, the study has the vibrancy and strength needed without having to rely on the whiteness of the paper as one would with watercolour. It will also remain wet enough to work in for the duration of the drawing. Charcoal is used to define direction and shape.

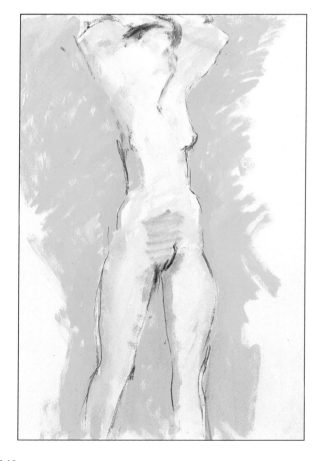

Cheryl Gould 'Flowers' 770 × 550mm (30 × 21½in.). This painting was carried out on a heavy watercolour paper. This forms a tough surface and also has a pleasing texture which holds brush marks well. The paint has been applied in a wide range of ways, from thin staining in places, building up to thick impasto. Flowers provide a good range of colours and tones, and although each flower shape is composed of small petal shapes, great care has been taken to ensure that the overall form of flowers is not lost.

143

Recommended kit

In order to complete the exercises and projects in this section, you will need:

Paints For the exercises and first project you will need the following oil colours: yellow ochre, raw sienna, raw umber, burnt umber (these can be Students' colours), alizarin crimson, cadmium red, cadmium yellow, cobalt blue, viridian green and flake white. For the second project you would probably need in addition light red, magenta, geranium rose, cadmium orange, lemon yellow, terre verte, cerulean blue, ultramarine, mauve, indian red and black.

Brushes Initially, you should have four bristle brushes – a No. 10 filbert and No. 10 flat, No. 6 round, and a No. 4 filbert – and one 'soft' brush for drawing in. A No. 3 mix of sable and ox or soft nylon is probably most suitable.

Knives A flat palette knife will be adequate for the first project, and a trowel type for the second. Either is suitable for the exercises.

Supports A pad of oil-sketching or painting paper (canvasette) is adequate for the exercises. For the first project, a Daler board is probably the most suitable support; for the second, hardboard (Masonite) or canvas board, or the largest size Daler board available (60 × 72cm/25 × 30in.), may be more appropriate.

Additional items An easel, either sketching or table, or failing that use the back of an old chair; a palette, either a ready-made wooden one, or one from glass, hardboard, plastic or paper, the important thing is to have a clean surface on which to lay out and mix your paints; rags for wiping; and a dipper or jar for turpentine.

A beginner's basic oil-painting kit.

Starting to paint

The list of materials given on pages 144–5 is fairly comprehensive and eventually you will certainly need most, if not all, of them. At the beginning, however, this is not necessary. The first really important thing to do in oil painting is to get the feel of the paint and enjoy the qualities that are specified to oil paint, and explore the range of marks you can make with your various brushes. The idea of carrying out exercises before you make a proper painting is rather like doing finger exercises in music, limbering up without the complication of trying to paint objects or a landscape.

At this stage, I would suggest a series of small exercises (say 15 × 15cm/6 × 6in.) exploring the qualities of the paint and surface. You may wish to expand on these and develop them in further exercises of your own.

You will need
☐ paints
☐ brushes
☐ painting knife
☐ a pad of oil-sketching paper or some Daler boards
☐ a palette
☐ a dipper (palette cup) containing turpentine
☐ rags

Use of brushes

Explore the range of marks that your brushes are capable of: this can either be in the form of a random doodle or a more organized chart which you can refer back to − it is really a matter of personal choice. The main object is to familiarize yourself with various brush marks. This will soon give you the confidence to select an appropriate brush for a particular task when you are working on a painting and will help you to enlarge your range of techniques.

The marks made by different brushes: (from top) flat, filbert, round, nylon and sable.

Laying out your palette

Obviously the way you lay out your palette is a matter of personal preference, but to enable you to work with more speed and fluency, it is advisable to establish an order for the colours on the palette, and stick to it. This will ensure that you can find them without having to spend time looking for them. The two small palettes illustrated here are laid out from warm to cool, with white as the divider, then the earth colours. One alternative would be to lay the colours out from light to dark, with white first, then moving through the colour range, as shown in the photograph of my palette.

My palette: white, raw sienna, naples yellow, cadmium yellow, lemon yellow, chrome yellow, cadmium orange, viridian, terre verte, emerald green, cinnabar green, chrome green, cerulean blue, alizarin crimson, magenta, cobalt violet, cadmium red, bright red, cobalt blue, ultramarine, black.

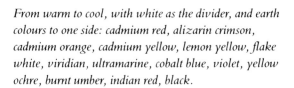

From warm to cool, with white as the divider, and earth colours to one side: cadmium red, alizarin crimson, cadmium orange, cadmium yellow, lemon yellow, flake white, viridian, ultramarine, cobalt blue, violet, yellow ochre, burnt umber, indian red, black.

Again from warm to cool, an extended palette: cadmium red, light red, crimson, magenta, geranium rose, cadmium orange, cadmium yellow, lemon yellow, viridian, terre verte, cerulean blue, cobalt blue, ultramarine, mauve, yellow ochre, burnt umber, indian red, black, flake white.

147

Colour

Although, at this stage, it is not necessary to go too deeply into colour theory, it is useful for the beginner to know about warm and cool colours. The phrase is used a great deal by artists when describing techniques or talking about the use of colour in a painting. The best place to start is with the colour wheel, a man-made device used to illustrate and explain colour theory. It is rather like a chart based on the colour spectrum found by passing light through a prism, but the important point to remember is that the artist is dealing with pigments which derive their colour through reflected, rather than direct, light.

The colour wheel illustrated is based on pigments. It was devised by Johannes Itten, who taught colour theory and practice to artists at the Bauhaus, in the 1930s. It starts with the three primary colours – red, yellow, and blue. These are pure colour and cannot be made by mixing together other pigments, but they do form the basis of the rest of the colour wheel. Surrounding these primaries are the secondary colours, which are a mixture of the primaries – red and yellow

produce orange, yellow and blue produce green, and red and blue give violet. The colours of the outer circle are known as tertiary colours. These are mixtures of the primary and secondary colours which give different strengths of colour. Red and orange, for example, will produce a red-orange, due to the predominance of the primary red in the two colours when mixed. Yellow and orange will produce a yellow-orange, and so on.

If the circle is divided in half, two groups of colour are formed – cool colours and warm colours. That is to say the colours of one half are warm in feeling compared with the rest of the colours which are cool in feeling. The word feeling is very important because it is an emotional response to the colours which makes us decide that they are warm or cool, although obviously there are associations within the range – reds, yellows and oranges make us think of fire, sun, heat, and so on, while in the cool range blues, greens and blue-violets make us think of sky, water and ice. This way of looking at colour is used extensively in the advertising industry where a particular mood or feeling is important.

Within the broad general terms 'warm' and 'cool', however, it is possible to find warmer and cooler variations – there are warmer greens and colder blues, and so on. A touch of red or violet in a blue will make it slightly warmer than a pure blue. These variations are infinite and very finely balanced. The degree of warmth or coolness also depends on the colours that surround a particular colour – chrome yellow placed next to lemon yellow will make the lemon yellow look cooler; viridian green next to lemon yellow will make the lemon yellow look warm.

There are examples of paintings which are predominantly warm or cool, and have been deliberately painted as such by the artists to convey a particular emotion to the spectator. In this way colour is as important as line or form in a composition. Specific use of warm or cool colours can also create a sense of space in a painting. You will notice in nature that distance tends to make

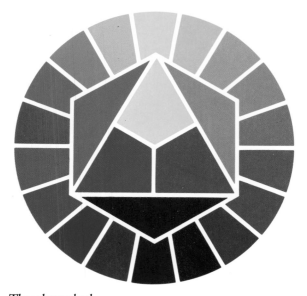

The colour wheel.

colours appear cooler – they take on a blue, hazy quality, because of the way the atmosphere affects how we see the colours. You will notice, however, that even in many old landscape paintings the artists used blues and other cool colours for backgrounds to create a feeling of distance, and warmer colours in the foreground to create the feeling of nearness. The Impressionists, too, used colour theory to create the feeling of light and vibrancy in their paintings. Today, abstract painters who may be unconcerned with any figurative elements in their works will achieve the feeling of space through their manipulation of colour theory.

Colour mixing

According to the colour wheel, it should be possible to produce all the colours you need from the primaries – red, yellow and blue. Unfortunately, this is not strictly true; there are some colours it is just not possible to create and the more intense violets, purples, greens and some blues have to come from a tube.

When you choose your oil colours you will find that there are various types of red, yellow and blue. It is very important to know the differences between them. Cadmium red, for example, is very near the primary red in the colour wheel. You will find that when you mix cadmium red with cadmium yellow you can achieve a good orange, near to the orange in the colour wheel. However if you use a crimson red with the cadmium yellow, the orange goes brown and the brilliance goes from it. The same applies with the yellows. Cadmium yellow is as good a primary as you will get, and mixed with cadmium red it gives a good orange, but lemon yellow will give a dull orange lacking in brightness.

These differences run through to the blues when mixed with reds. Our primary red (the cadmium), when mixed with cobalt blue, according to the colour circle should give us a good violet, but it will in fact make brown. To achieve violet, mix crimson red with blue.

Practise mixing colours so that you begin to get the feel of how the various pigments will react together and the colours you can make: (from top) cadmium red + cadmium yellow (this is a 'true' orange); cadmium red + lemon yellow; crimson red + cadmium yellow; crimson red + lemon yellow; cobalt blue + cadmium yellow (the 'truest' green); cobalt blue + lemon yellow; crimson red + cobalt blue (a 'true' violet); and cadmium red + cobalt blue.

149

Mixing primary and secondary complementaries plus increasing amounts of white. Orange and cobalt blue make a cool grey, violet and cadmium yellow, and green and cadmium red make warm greys, almost flesh tints.

It is useful at this stage to try small mixes of these colours and note the different results for future reference. The more you play with your paints and become familiar with the way they behave, the quicker you build up a knowledge which will become second nature as you work.

Wet into wet

There are many examples of the use of this technique, most often by abstract painters. It is an exciting way to explore the qualities, properties and possibilities of oil paint.

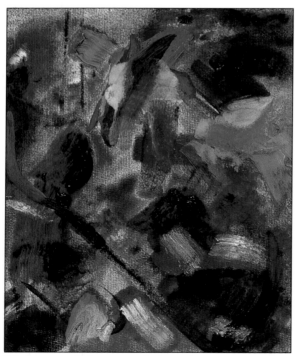

Wet into wet, thick paint worked into thin.

Mix a small quantity of thin paint to the consistency of watercolour. Then lay it on the surface quite freely. While this is still wet, add some thicker paint, of another colour, into the wet surface, perhaps scrubbing it around with a brush in some areas.

You will notice that the colour tends to bleed into the wet background, giving soft fuzzy edges in the areas where it is thinnest. Where it is slightly thicker, it will sit on top of the surface. You can also see how the colours will intermix on the surface in varying degrees of intensity.

Overall, this method gives a soft, translucent quality to the shapes, and a magical atmosphere and almost dreamlike aspect to the paint. In the areas where the paint is thicker, it seems to have a depth to it.

Glazing

Glazing is a very useful technique in many ways. It will give parts of a painting a rich glowing effect, and can also be used to overpaint and unify areas without having to repaint them totally.

Prepare an area of solid random shapes and let them dry off – this should take about 24 hours. When the paint is dry, overlay thin transparent paint of different colours. Use a soft brush for this so that you avoid any brush marks. The thinness of the overpainting will allow the colour beneath the glazed paint to show through, and it is this that gives the glowing effect to the painting.

You will notice that the colours have a brilliance which can only be achieved in this way. A green which is painted over a more solid area of green and blue, for example, intensifies in richness;

150

GLAZING

1 Green glazed over yellow tends to become sharper and brighter.

2 Blue over yellow. The colours mix on the surface, not on the palette.

3 Yellow over blue; yellow over darker colours often appears more solid.

4 Areas of purple glazed over other colours enhance the feeling of space.

Glazed colours have a unique brilliance.

painted over bright yellow, it becomes sharper and brighter. This is also true of the reds and blues.

The colours used for the solid shapes in this example have been thinned down and overlaid across each other. It is interesting to note that some colours, like the yellow, when painted over darker shapes, actually appear more solid – this can be seen, for instance, on the green and purple shapes. This overlaying can also enhance the feeling of space; even in this small exercise, the special aspect has emerged quite naturally.

151

Dragged brush techniques

In this exercise, keep the paint fairly thick and stiff in consistency. Start by dragging the brush strokes across the surface, noticing the texture made by the brush and surface together. Also, mix the brush marks together, enjoying the feeling of fluidity of the thick wet paint.

While this is drying, drag some more paint over the surface of the brush marks. You will find that the wet paint will move uncontrollably. This effect can be used consciously in your paintings.

You will also notice that the paint sticks to the raised texture and gives a gritty or dry feeling. It can also add a sparkle to the surface, and gives a completely different effect from the previous exercise. This sparkle can be very useful in the finishing stages of a painting.

Using a painting knife

Many people find thick paint more exciting to work with than thin, and the element of chance involved in knife painting – it is not so controllable as a brush mark – is in itself stimulating to many artists.

There are many ways to use a painting knife. The paint can be laid on to the surface very thickly to lose the surface texture of the ground

Paint dragged over surface brush marks.

completely. Alternatively, it can be lightly scraped or dragged over the surface to create a broken, sparkling feeling. It can also be used in conjunction with a brush. The contrast of marks adds extra interest.

The colour lies on the surface of the canvas or board in a different way from paint that is brushed on and there are no brush marks. The paint also usually has sharper edges than you could achieve with a brush.

There are many examples of well-known artists who have made extensive use of the knife in their paintings; a notable example is John Constable.

KNIFE PAINTING

1 Using the edge of the knife will give a sharp linear mark.

2 Using the whole blade flat allows a full gestural movement.

3 Knife painting gives a surface free from brush marks.

SCUMBLING

A colour scumbled over the support will mean areas of the white ground will show through.

Scumbling light over dark, the previous colour is still visible and changes the lighter colour.

Dark over light – the eye tends to mix the colours on the surface of the painting.

Scumbling

Scumbling is applying thick paint loosely and freely over the surface of a painting. It can be used to add interest to large plain areas of work, it can also give a glowing effect to the surface, tone down passages of a painting, produce a softness in places, and can add freshness and light.

Scumbling can be used on a surface that is already painted, or applied over an untinted ground. The colour underneath the scumble will show through. This gives an exciting broken, dappled effect. Different effects can be achieved, according to whether the scumble is lighter or darker than the ground. Also, depending on the colours you use, laying broken colours over one another can mean that the eye will mix the colours on the surface of the painting.

You can achieve interesting effects by scumbling the paint on with a rag or tissue, rather than a brush. This can give a variety of textures and effects to the surface of the painting.

The doodle

The doodle incorporates all or most of the elements in the smaller single exercises. The advantage of it is that the elements all interact and the various qualities complement each other. The only organization I allowed myself was that on one side the colour is thin and transparent in feeling, and on the other side the paint is thick and gestural with more intermixing of the colours and white so that you notice the subtle tonal variation. What is also interesting in this doodle is the quality of the thin transparent paints. They seem to float and create space and distance of a different kind from the thicker areas.

The way to learn from this exercise and also the smaller ones is to stop and really examine what you have done. At this stage, there will be a good many accidental qualities which are sometimes quite magical and can be used and made to work for you in a more considered situation later on.

The elements of the doodle interact with each other.

153

Project: A still life 1

The simple still-life group is an excellent way for the newcomer to oil painting to experiment and learn about the medium. By working indoors, you don't have all the problems encountered outside, such as changing light, and unwanted spectators. At this stage, it is more important to learn to manipulate the paint and experiment with different brushes and ways of applying the paint. It is only by doing this that you find the ways that suit you best and develop your own technique, which eventually becomes as personal and unique as handwriting. For this painting, I will show how to build from thin paint to thick in one sitting. By keeping the first areas thinly painted, the surface remains in a good state to make alterations and adjustments.

You will need
- paints
- brushes
- painting knife
- a Daler board, about 40 × 50cm (16 × 20in.)
- a palette
- a dipper (palette cup) containing turpentine
- rags
- a pencil and cartridge (drawing) paper

The still-life arrangement of objects.

Choice of subject

For this first project, I have set up a very simple still life using objects that are easily found around the home. Coloured paper creates areas of tone and colour in the simplest possible way. This avoids the complexities of folds and texture which you will find with drapery.

I have used the fruit and the plate because of their simplicity of shape. All are almost round, but have the variation and subtlety of colour needed to help you to see the changes of colour and tone in an individual object. You will also notice here that there is a relationship of colour which connects the objects and background throughout the picture. The predominant colour is established by the green background. The colour then ranges through a variety of greens in the apples and bottle, working its way through to the palest apple which is almost yellow to the full yellow of the lemon. Then, from the yellow of the lemon it is a natural step to the yellow–orange and full orange of the oranges themselves which intensify into the reds of the red apple. The blue of the small piece of drapery seems to act as an accent due to its opposition to the orange colour. I used the egg because of its simple smooth shape which when placed on the blue seemed to pick up the blues and grey–pinks of the colours around it.

Preliminary sketches

The viewpoint I have chosen is a flat and straight on view. This means that there are almost no perspective problems. It is a good idea before you start to make one or two very simple sketches just to get the composition right. As you will see from the first little drawing that I made, the composition was not satisfactory. The bottle and plate were practically central to the picture, thus creating a rather obvious viewpoint, but moving this focus over to the right of centre and adding the light strip to the left-hand side achieves a better balance and more interest. This will only take a few minutes of your time but it is invaluable when planning your picture.

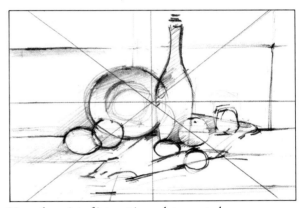

Here, the point of interest is much too central.

Moving the bottle makes a more interesting grouping.

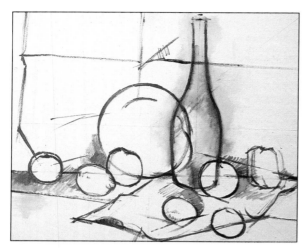

The initial drawing in in raw umber.

Painting areas of background.

Paint areas of light and dark together.

When sketching in your composition on your board, use the minimum amount of drawing. Remember that almost all of the drawing will eventually be covered up. You only need to indicate, as accurately as possible, the sizes and shapes of the objects and their relationship to each other. Draw with sable using a neutral colour, in this case I used raw umber. The first drawn lines can be sketched in in pencil before the paint is used. Charcoal is sometimes used, but it tends to mix in with the first application of paint, which could present problems for the beginner.

I arranged my group of objects so that the light source comes into the picture from the side; this enhances the dramatic effect of light and dark and, more importantly for the beginner, it simplifies the way we see the forms. You will find that when you come to paint out of doors, the light source can present difficult handling problems (see pages 171-2), particularly if you work on a single painting all day, as the light is constantly changing. It requires a good deal of skill to organize the pace and tone of the picture right from the start to take this into account.

Painting the background
The second stage of the painting is to paint in thinly and in a general way the broad areas of colour and tone, letting the drawing show through. Don't worry about the colours overlapping, and don't try to paint each object separately – remember that it is the whole of the painting that you are concerned with. Use fairly large brushes so that you keep the surface free in feeling. This will also stop you fiddling with small details at this early stage.

I started with the background first only because it is the largest single area, but once a general statement was made, I quickly moved on to the smaller areas. It is important to try and paint these together, by that I mean if you are painting one area of the plate, you will look and make a decision regarding the colour and tone of a corresponding area next to it, which might be the bottle or background. In this way, the whole painting will gradually build up and you will avoid painting objects singularly. Paint lights and darks together, this will help you to make judgements as to the relative value of light and dark. You will also notice that although there are colour changes, as in the green pepper next to the blue drapery, the tones at their darkest are about the same. This is also true of the oranges and apples and the corresponding backgrounds. This is an important point to learn. While colours may change, tones may well come together. This is what will give a painting atmosphere and will get away from the feeling that the objects exist completely separately.

Re-establishing the drawing

You will probably find at this stage that some of the drawing has either got lost (because you have painted over it) or gone wrong in the painting. Don't worry about this – it happens in the course of a painting. All it means is that at this stage it is a good idea to re-establish the drawing in those areas where you feel it needs it. I found in this painting that it was necessary to re-draw the bottle and refine its shape, which had become clumsy. The fruit was also generally too round and was beginning to lose its character. I was able to change these without difficulty because I had kept the paint loose and thin, and like this it is easily overpainted.

The first details

By this stage, I am being more specific and looking in more detail at shapes and the small colour changes within the objects, paying particular attention to the way the colours reflect the different colours around them. You can see that I have carried some of the warmth of the orange on the left of the lemon into the lemon itself, so that a part of the lemon is almost orange. The orange also reflects down on to the surface of the table, giving off a warmer half-tone around it. The lemon was a particularly good choice for this

Initial areas of colour scrubbed in.

The drawing has now been re-established.

The fruit lends warm tones to the table.

Thicker paint is used in the lighter areas.

Almost all the board is now covered.

project because as you will see it seems to pick up a great deal of the colour around it – greens, oranges and browns.

I am now able to use thicker paint, particularly in the light areas. The heavier paint strokes seem to give a feeling of surfaces reflecting light while the thin dark areas give a feeling of shadow.

I have kept the paint thinner on the bottle to give more of the feeling of transparency of glass and only where the light is reflected have I allowed the paint to become thicker. In this last stage, I have defined some of the lines of the composition more fully. For example, the folds on the green background paper are important directional lines and the light shape of the wall is crucial to the balance of the composition, particularly where the light meets the dark of the table and orange. This

creates an accent and seems to balance the picture more satisfactorily. I have also found that the brightness of the orange at that point is useful in bringing the eye over to that side of the painting.

Adding the highlights

It is at this final stage that I have started to look at the highlights or lightest parts of the objects. I have carefully avoided adding these until now since they require a good deal of thought and restraint. You will find that there is a great temptation to over-emphasize the highlights and add flecks of white all over the place. When this occurs in a picture, these highlights usually look as though they are on the surface of the painting rather than on the objects themselves; in other words, they look totally unrelated to the whole.

Being more specific about edges.

Beginning to look at the lightest areas.

Building up the highlights.

Try to see highlights as areas of lightness of colour rather than as white reflections. I have noticed by now that the lightest points in the picture are the lemon, part of the apple next to it, the strip down the left-hand side, and the egg. All the other tones gradually come closer together so that the picture is predominantly dark and half-tones. This gives a bit of drama to the objects but, more importantly, if you can learn to look at your painting in this way, trying to sum up its whole feeling, stage by stage, you will find that you will begin to do this before you actually start painting. You will begin to apply this same sort of looking to the objects themselves.

This part of the apple is one of the lightest areas of the whole painting.

159

Underpainting

In all the little exercises that you carried out, and in the first project, you will have noticed that the paint has stayed wet for a considerable length of time, probably all day. This is one of the basic qualities of oil paint, which gives it the advantage over water-based pigments of being flexible for change and alteration over a long period. There are two basic methods of working in oils. The first, which is the approach taken in the first project, is called *alla prima*. This simply means working the paint directly on to the canvas into wet paint. The colour is mixed on the canvas as well as on the palette. This way of working is the most usual when you are doing a painting at one sitting – a landscape, for instance – when you can only spend a short time working, or a portrait where your time is limited to a day or part of a day. The second method is a more considered approach in that you have to have decided on the relative tones of the areas of the canvas or board before you start to paint. This is a very structured approach to picture-making and requires a good deal of time and a strong idea of how the paint will look to be successful.

> **You will need**
> ☐ paints
> ☐ brushes
> ☐ oil-sketching paper or a Daler board
> ☐ a palette
> ☐ a dipper (palette cup) containing turpentine
> ☐ rags

Ken Howard 'Homage to Sir William Orpen' 1500 × 1350mm (60 × 50in.). This picture is a beautiful example of underpainting cool greys and whites with a warm colour. You can see the full orange on the vertical edges of the picture. The colour filters through giving a vibrancy to the cool areas and cleverly lead us to the warm tones of the head and hands.

Underpainting technique

This approach to oil painting has a strong tradition. The picture is usually begun with a more detailed drawing than in *alla prima* painting on the canvas, and is then built up in a variety of ways. Sometimes strong glazes are laid on top of the drawing and when they are dry, they are worked into with thicker paint, and perhaps over-glazed again.

The whole of this method can be carried out on the white ground, although some artists prefer to stain the ground with a colour to give extra vibrancy to the colours applied later. The colour chosen to stain the surface ground can either set the mood of the picture from the start (either warm or cool), or act as a contrast to the colours added as the painting continues.

Thinned oil paint is usually used for underpainting, although some artists use acrylics, which dry quickly.

Monochrome underpainting

There is a further way of starting a painting, called underpainting in monochrome (monochrome meaning one colour). The reason for underpainting in this way is broadly to create the light and dark areas and build up the three-dimensional aspect of your picture before using colour. It is best to use a neutral colour (in the example illustrated here I used burnt umber and blue), since these have the advantage of drying quickly. Don't add white but thin the pigment down with turpentine, almost to the consistency of watercolour. For the areas you wish to be light in the finished painting, leave the ground white, and build up the layers of pigment for the darkest areas of your painting. In this way you will create the light and dark tonal areas.

UNDERPAINTING IN MONOCHROME

1 Drawing in the main lines and directions using burnt umber, or raw umber. Remember to keep the drawing as simple as possible.

2 The next stage is to lay in quickly a thin wash of paint to indicate the feeling of shape and tone.

3 Here, I am starting to vary the lights and darks of the trees, keeping a general feeling of shape to preserve the dramatic quality of the trees.

4 Colour is now introduced on to the tonal underpainting; the tone of the colour relates to the first underpainting.

Project: A still life 2

One of the outstanding advantages of painting still lifes is that you, the artist, are in complete control. You select the format, and choose and arrange the objects right from the start. You could say that it is at this point that the painting really begins. It is always a good idea to make your choice with a theme in mind. This could be the relationship of colour running through the objects and background, maybe a range of predominantly warm or cool colours. Shape could also be a strong element, for example, the linking of curved lines throughout, or the

The more complex still-life arrangement for this project allows a larger format.

contrast of curves against straight lines, which will often produce a dramatic effect in a composition. The use of texture in a painting heightens the feeling of surfaces – this can be achieved by contrasting textural qualities within the picture, such as drapery with glass, or a piece of natural form such as bark against paper or metal. Try to avoid the idea of a picture telling a story by using objects that are only connected in the literal sense. Remember that the picture's strength lies in its composition and colour. If there is another connection, it will be secondary to these considerations. There is such a wide choice of approaches open to the artist that it is only by experimenting that you will begin to develop your own ideas about the sort of image you prefer.

> **You will need**
> ■ paints, extended colour range
> ■ brushes
> ■ trowel-type painting knife
> ■ hardboard or canvas board, 65 × 75cm (26 × 30in.)
> ■ a palette
> ■ a dipper (palette cup) containing turpentine
> ■ rags

Choice of objects

The format for this second still life is larger than the first, which will allow me to make a more complex grouping of objects and be more adventurous in the way the objects are arranged. Instead of flat areas of colour as in the first project, here I have used drapery, the folds of which will give me strong directional lines running through the composition. I have used fruit again because of its colour content and the way it naturally seems to relate to the colours surrounding it. The plant is an important element. Apart from being an exciting organic shape, it encompasses a great deal of the colour that occurs in the rest of the painting. Also, its overall shape and tone, seen against the light background, help to balance the strong red area on the right of the picture. The sheep's skull in the foreground is also an object which picks up all the subtle half-tones and greys of the colours around it.

I also incorporated objects with reflective surfaces – the bottle and metal fruit stand. Finally, I used the check-patterned cloth to create interest in the foreground area; this helps to give a feeling of space because of the way the checks diminish in size as they recede through the picture.

When choosing objects, try to select them from the point of view of colour and see if you can trace links of colour between them. All the objects I have chosen have these colour links, from the warm reds of the drapery and fruit through to the orange and orange-yellows of the orange and apples, then to the full yellow of the grapefruit and the green of the apples and bottle. The green of the plant is moving towards the blue of the cloth. The aubergine (eggplant) acts as a focal point of colour, because its purple quality forms a link between the blue and the red. Choice of colour is also important in creating a sense of rhythm in a composition. A good sense of rhythm means that the eye will travel through the picture from one area to another, guided by the juxtapositions between them as they overlap and cross each other. In this way, painters control how you look at their pictures, perhaps leading you gently to an important focal point.

If you consciously think in these terms when you paint, you will find that it quickly becomes second nature and it will form part of your intuitive colour sense. This applies to landscape or any other form of painting; you will see these links in almost everything in the course of everyday life, whether you are painting or not.

Choice of eye level

It is advisable for the beginner to choose an eye level either straight on or just above; in other words, if the group is set up at table height you either stand or sit to paint. If you set the group up on the floor, although visually exciting, you will create drawing problems, such as foreshortening, which at this stage are best avoided. Here, by taking a slightly higher eye level than in the first still life more of the picture surface is broken up by shape and colour.

Arranging and lighting your objects

When arranging your composition you need to consider shape, not just the shapes of the individual elements but the shape of the spaces between them. These areas are called negative shapes. They are often ignored by beginners, although they are just as important as the objects themselves. If you think of the flat surface of the picture, and then think of the pattern quality of the drawing on that surface, you can realize that the negative shapes play an important part in the whole design. You will select objects for your painting for a number of reasons, one of which will probably be that they have interesting shapes, so it should follow that all the shapes created in the picture are as interesting as possible. Lighting can also help in describing the shapes and forms of your objects. The light source can heighten the dramatic effect of a picture by casting strong dark shadows. On the other hand, a strong overall light can achieve a brilliant sparkling effect, with areas of intense highlights.

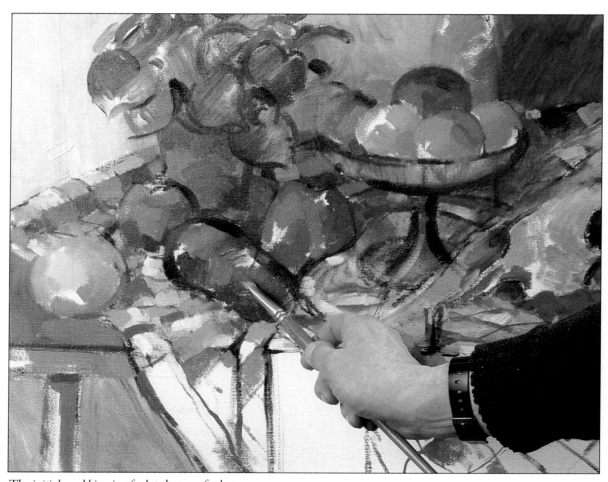

The initial scrubbing in of related areas of colour.

Initial stages

The start of the painting was the same as in the first still life, except that as the grouping was more complicated, I sketched in very lightly in pencil before making my first drawn marks in paint. This gave me more flexibility when trying to arrive at a satisfactory composition. At this stage, the painting has been kept very broad, with the paint as thin as possible, so that should I need to make changes, it will be very easy to wipe or scrape clean. You will notice that although the plant is made up of a number of elements, I have deliberately seen it as a simple overall shape and painted it loosely, rather than getting involved with the individual shapes themselves. This will come at a later stage.

The painting at this stage is very broad.

Covering the canvas

It is also important at this early stage to try to relate the tones and colours as closely as you can, although they will almost certainly be altered and adjusted as the painting progresses. Most of the canvas is covered by now and statements of colour and tone have been made regarding all the objects and their surroundings. The only outstanding area is the checked cloth; this requires more time due to the formal nature of the pattern and needs to be drawn with some accuracy. The important thing at this stage is to establish the mood and atmosphere of the picture; this is usually through the colour and tonal relationships.

The fruit stand reflects colour around it.

The first details

By now, I am beginning to look in more detail at individual parts of the painting. The metal fruit stand as well as the area surrounding its base show how reflective surfaces provide a wide range of colours, but you must beware of and try to avoid the temptation to over-state the highlights. At this point it is more important to see how the tones are very closely related to each other and the edges almost disappear into shadow. I have also developed the other parts of the picture, notably the skull and the fruit on the stand.

Form and colour are now developing.

Looking in more detail at the fruit stand.

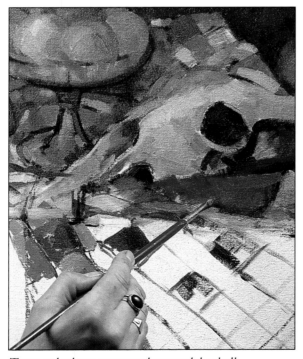

Tones and colours come together round the skull.

At this stage, I am more confident of colour and tone.

Colour and tonal relationships

It may be necessary at this point to re-establish the drawing in certain areas. At this stage, I am looking at the colours in the fruit stand and how they reflect into each other and change the nature of orange and yellow. You can see how the very yellow apple has taken into its shadow the orange quality of the orange fruit next to it. I am beginning to use thicker paint now, because I am confident about the colour and tonal relationships and I know that some of my marks will remain unchanged throughout the painting of the picture.

It can be seen by looking at the sheep's skull in the picture how all the subtle tones and colours seem to come together in this form. Because it is the lightest object in the group, it absorbs many of the shades surrounding it, and we can see the wonderful variety of greys which occur on the surface, warm pinky greys moving into cool green-blue greys.

Warm and cool areas

I am now working on the left-hand side of the picture. The grapefruit is an important element in the balance of the composition. The bright yellow helps to counterbalance the dark red passage in the opposite side of the picture, so the degree of

The brightness of the grapefruit is critical.

brightness is critical. If I make it too light, it will stand out too much; if I understate it, the point of it in the composition will be lost. The only immediate part of the painting which connects with it from the point of view of colour is the table top which has the same warm glow. It is also surrounded by a contrasting cool blue, so I have to relate the yellow to these colours. To do this, I notice that some of the yellow reflects down into the table top and there are areas of the yellow which take on a greeny quality which helps to bridge the gap from blue to yellow, as well as forming a link with the green apple just beyond.

At this stage, I am also beginning to paint into the checked cloth. At first sight, I am sure this complicated cloth pattern can appear daunting to the beginner, but don't be put off from using pattern in your pictures just because you feel it is too difficult. They create interesting and exciting areas in the picture, as well as being very useful in terms of composition. The best approach is to paint what you see, for instance, if you have an area of dark which is made because of the dark checks, just paint them. Don't think of them as checks, just as areas where you see definite patterns of light and dark, then it is easy to draw and paint them. If you look closely at parts of my

painting you will find it hard to define precisely the check pattern, but because it is well defined in other areas, you willingly accept that the pattern runs all through the picture, even though it can't always be seen in a precise way.

Establishing the planes

At this stage, I have drawn the cloth pattern more accurately with a fine brush, and I shall now be looking closely at the way the blues change. There are basically three blues, the dark blue, lighter blue and the blue-grey. Once the formal layout has been understood, the most important aspect is how they change due to the folds and how they describe the horizontal plane of the table top and the vertical plane down the front of the table. You will notice that I am developing the front edge of the table where this change in direction takes place. The light falls mainly from above and to the side so the top plane of the table is light. I have therefore emphasized this edge by making the white checks on the top surface strong where they change direction and become darker on the vertical drop.

More detailed work on the cloth.

167

Balance and movement

By now I feel that it is necessary to work on the plant. This, like the grapefruit, is an important compositional element. It is important as an overall shape to balance the picture. This is achieved by the contrast in tone of dark on light and its mauve-red flowers form a link with the red drapery. This link is helped by the red of the bottle top and the red apple in the fruit stand leading the eye over to the red drapery. I am now also developing the drawing of the leaf shapes, keeping the tones close together so as not to break down the overall feeling of the plant. The sharp pointed nature of the flowers takes the eye up from the busy lower half of the picture and helps to create movement through the composition.

The folds of drapery are almost completed.

The plant is an important element in balancing the picture.

Finishing touches

As the picture is nearing completion, it is important to stop and have a good look at the whole painting so far to see if there are any parts which are not working – the drawing might need re-establishing or it might be that certain parts have become over-stated or under-stated. In my painting, at this point, I can see that the orange on the right-hand side against the red appears to be jumping forward in the picture. I could re-paint it so that it recedes, or I could try glazing it down. This is, in fact, what I have done. By glazing thin red paint over the painted orange I was able to pull it back into the drapery. I left the very centre of the orange showing through so that the edges almost disappeared. I then lightened the horn of the sheep's skull to bring it forward. It was also at this point that I painted some detail into the fruit stand and finished off the check pattern. I also felt that the table top needed lightening to give more contrast with the dark shadow underneath. This helps to bring that edge forward.

Because the light background is a large plain area I painted some of the soft tones with a palette knife to give the area a textural interest, without making it too prominent.

Glazing the orange pulls it back into the drapery.

Varnishing pictures

Varnishes are used for two main reasons. The first, and most important, is to protect the painted surface from damage caused by atmospheric pollution, which can cause discoloration and eventually do irreparable harm to the pigments themselves, and from minor scratches and marks. Secondly, varnishes are used to restore the original quality of colour and tone to your picture.

You will probably have noticed during the course of your work on the exercises and projects that in many cases the colour has gone dull or patchy. This is due to the way some colours dry. If they have plenty of oil ground with them they will probably stay shiny; if you have mixed a lot of turpentine with your paint it will probably have dried dull and matt. This patchy quality is irritating and distracting. To overcome it, you can use re-touching varnish. This is an ideal temporary measure and can be used straight away to restore the brilliance of the paint.

In the longer term, however, a clear picture varnish will be necessary, although you shouldn't apply this for at least nine months to a year after the picture has been completed, since it takes this amount of time for the paint to dry and harden fully. If varnish is applied before the paint is fully dry, cracking or crazing will almost certainly occur, due to the different drying times of the paint and varnish.

When you come to apply the picture varnish make sure that your painting is clean and free from dust particles. To do this, wash it gently with a soft rag or cottonwool (absorbent cotton) dipped in mild soapy water, then rinse the rag with clean water and go over the surface again to get rid of all the soap. Let it dry thoroughly. Apply the varnish with a soft varnish brush, which can be obtained from art suppliers. Start from the top and apply the varnish thinly and evenly over the whole surface at one go. If you allow one area of varnish to dry and then continue you will find that there is an edge where the two varnished layers overlap.

Subjects for the oil painter

The choice of subject for the painter is endless and what moves one person to paint a particular subject will not necessarily have the same effect on another. It is, however, a strange phenomenon about painting that someone else's interpretation of a subject which is not particularly to our liking can have the power to move us – it is not so much what you paint as how you interpret the subject. If you are drawn to a subject, do not be put off by what might seem like problems at the time, have a go. You will find that your enthusiasm will help you to surmount many of the technical difficulties, and, the more you do it, the more your technique will improve.

Oil is very suitable for many subjects for the beginner due to its flexibility. If a painting is going wrong, or proving difficult, oil will allow you to scrape or rub it off the surface and rework it again and again. The technique is obviously different from, say, watercolour, which requires a more careful and considered approach, and won't allow for much pushing around the surface. Scale also plays a part. Very large watercolours require technical know-how and time, whereas a fairly large oil painting can be tackled more readily by an enthusiastic beginner.

John Constable 'Sketch for Leaping Horses' 1294 × 1880mm (51 × 71in.). This full-size sketch shows how Constable ironed out many of the problems of composition and colour before he committed himself to the final painting. Although this is referred to as a sketch, this only means that it was a loosely painted preparatory work – it has all the completeness of a finished painting.

Ken Howard 'Studio Interior' 625 × 750mm (25 × 30in.). This painting of Ken Howard's is an interesting example which shows that one does not necessarily have to go far for subjects. Very often the immediate environment in which you live and work can be just as stimulating pictorially as anything which you deliberately search out.

Painting out of doors

Although as we have seen, the simple still-life group is an excellent way for the newcomer to oil painting to experiment and learn about the medium, sooner or later many people (probably the majority) will feel that landscape is the subject that inspires them to want to paint most of all. So, the problems which I have outlined – light, spectators, and so on – will eventually have to be faced; the early work at home will have prepared you with the basic use of oil painting materials and the medium itself.

A clear advantage of working directly from nature is that you can compile a selection of studies of a location or subject and build them into a more considered composition. This also allows you to increase the scale to a size that would not be possible out of doors. There are many examples of this way of working. Constable made endless colour studies and drawings which he then developed into full-size sketches, then turned these into a finished painting.

The problem of light can be approached in several ways. Usually if you start painting out of doors and you intend to spend the best part of the day at it, you can assume that choosing your subject and the initial drawing will take an hour or so. During the time spent drawing and blocking in the large masses, you will not have to make major decisions about the light, except to bear in mind that it is changing very slowly. When you come to make specific decisions, save them until you are well on into the painting. Details can also be left until near the end as often the overall light won't affect how you paint them greatly.

Another way of dealing with the light is to paint on a small scale and do several paintings in a

This study is formed by the rather warm sultry day making dark shadows which push the white screens in to dramatic prominence.

The paint in this picture varies from very thin to thicker light scumbling in the sky area to convey the light misty atmosphere of this kind of subject.

day. By doing this, you will gradually begin to catch the light and build up a series of little paintings, telling the story of the changing light over a period of time. It would then be interesting to compare how changes in light affect the feeling of the landscape over the period of a day.

If the weather is fine and sunny you will notice that the paint, especially if you put it on thinly, will dry off more quickly than indoors. This is one of the major advantages of working outside.

There are also logistical problems to working out of doors. It is advisable to keep equipment down to the absolute essentials. Make sure that the size of canvas or board is one that you can

handle – remember that you are going to be going home with a wet painting so it has to be easy to carry. Art shops sell special carrying straps for wet paintings. As for the critical spectators, well you just have to learn to live with them.

Alternatively, it is nearly always possible to paint from a window or in your garden. The window can give the picture an extra dimension, since by including it as part of the composition you convey the feeling of looking through a vista. The garden has certain advantages: you can go where you like, you can always be sure of getting the same spot again, and you can spend as much time as you wish on the painting.

This little study was carried out on a piece of mounting card, one of many oil sketches made on the spot. Obviously it is necessary to work fast with a subject like a sunset so I have kept the scale small and the paint is very thin and washy in places.

Using photographs

You might prefer to paint portraits of people or animals, although they always pose a problem simply because they move. This is where a camera can be a useful aid. I use the word 'aid' deliberately, as there does not seem much point in taking a photograph and just reproducing in paint what was probably better as a photograph anyway! But there are times when certain information is needed, either as a supplement to a drawing, or as a way to capture quickly the feeling that you want in the picture. This, combined with quick sketches, will give added information for you to use.

Photographs can also provide the stimulus for an idea. The photograph reproduced here, for example, was taken by me on a walk in Wales. I was attracted by the colour of the moss-grown stump which was bright green, and the odd, interesting shapes of the decaying wood surrounded by spiky brambles and roots. Although I had the photograph to work from, my first impressions and memories of that encounter were more important as they formed the basis of the idea for the painting. I first made several small scribbles on paper, trying to formulate my idea. The next stage was to make a larger, more detailed drawing, working towards that precise composition. This I carried out in colour, using paint and inks. You will see that the picture has now moved away from the photograph: the basic composition has changed, and the colour is also changing. I have heightened the green of the stump and, to emphasize this, I have introduced the orange.

The photograph is now totally discarded as my drawing is to form the basis of the projected painting. I began to realize that the shapes had a sinister, almost animal-like, quality to them which was not in the photograph. This aspect I developed further in the painting. You will also see that the final painting differs from the drawing in many ways. It is not just a question of doing a

The photograph that was the starting point for the painting below.

The detailed colour drawing.

The finished painting.

painting of the drawing – there must be room for development in the painting itself. I have retained the feeling of the dark woodland but there is almost a feeling of a fantastic stage set emerging which is far from the original photograph. In this sequence I have tried to show that there are ways of working from photographs that are more than just copying them.

Painting from sketches

One of the most enjoyable and satisfying ways to acquire subjects for oil paintings is through using a sketchbook. You should never be without one, either at work or at home – think of it as a visual notebook. When you see a subject that you find interesting, jot it down. Drawings made on holiday, or on a normal day-to-day basis, will provide endless material for paintings carried out in the studio. (They will also help you to improve your drawing technique.) Obviously making the sketch studies is the first step, but when you are sketching you do not always have a finished painting in mind. So, how do you set about translating a drawing from your sketchbook into a finished painting?

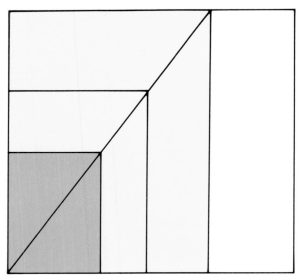

Any of the rectangles is in proportion to the original sketch.

Your first consideration will be to compose that initial sketch into a pleasing and well-constructed picture. You will also probably find that your first sketch is a different shape from the final format you have in mind, so you will have to alter or 'translate' your sketch to fit your new shape. The easiest way to do this is to redraw the main shapes and directions of your sketch on to another piece of paper, altering and adjusting them until you arrive at the arrangement that is most satisfying to you, and seems to work best.

The next stage is to transfer this image on to the larger shape that is to be your finished painting. For this, a system called 'gridding up' or 'squaring up' is used. This is simple to carry out. First, make sure that your small study is the same proportion as the painting is going to be. An easy method of reproducing the exact proportion from a small scale to a larger one is to lay the small shape (your drawing) on to the larger area (your painting support) tight into a corner and draw a diagonal line through the small shape, continuing it until it meets the edge of the painting support. Any rectangle drawn with that same diagonal will be in direct proportion to your smaller shape, and the area outside the point where it strikes the edge is waste. In the illustration here, any one of the coloured rectangles would be in direct proportion to the original drawing.

Having settled on the scale and proportion of your painting, you now need to transfer the drawing to the painting surface. To do this, you impose a grid structure on top of your study by drawing in two diagonals from corner to corner, then dividing it horizontally and vertically into four equal rectangles. This grid can then be subdivided as many times as you wish just by halving the shapes diagonally, horizontally and vertically. The number of times you repeat the process, obviously, depends on the complexity of the drawing you are transferring; the more detail you have the more reference points you will need. You will probably find it helps to number the grid lines.

The final step is to repeat this grid-making process on your painting support. You will now have a series of grid lines which correspond exactly to your small grid. These are the reference points which will enable you to transfer the marks from your small drawing to your final picture.

This is a pen and wash drawing made on the spot for a later painting. There are some colour notes on the actual sketch – this is often a useful addition to drawings made outside.

This small version of the original drawing has been made to improve the composition. The adjustments here are minor, mainly to give more room for the sky; this slightly increases the feeling of distance.

The drawing on to the support – in this case, hardboard (Masonite) – has been kept very simple. Just outlining the main shapes and directions is all that is needed at this stage, the rest will come with the painting.

Composing a picture

The important thing to remember about painting is that it is not just about technical skill and knowledge. You learn and develop your skills in order to convey the excitement you feel through painting. In the first two projects I dealt with painting a picture in a fairly objective way through still life, which has involved composition, colour, and, most of all, looking. Here, I shall deal with putting together a picture from various elements to make an imaginative composition. The picture I have decided to use as an example is totally different from the previous ones in subject matter and intention. Nevertheless, the considerations which are made have a great deal in common with those involved in the first two projects.

Sketchbook drawing for the eagle's head.

Problems of scale

The first point to note is the picture's scale and size. This picture is painted on a large format; this is an important step away from the first two pictures which were both small scale. The reason I make a point of this is that when you up the scale, there has to be much more information contained in the forms. The first two pictures were composed of small objects – fruit, and so on. Now we are dealing with large human figures – almost life size in the foreground – and a large space from front to back of the picture. The foreground figure occupies almost half of the picture space. One of the main pictorial problems was to relate the foreground figure to the background figure in a space almost devoid of objects. This has been done by the use of directional lines and points throughout the picture, and the direction of the figure's arms, which is echoed by the line of the square red shape at the top as well as the direction of the bottom line of the same red shape echoed again by the line of her breasts. These imaginary and real lines direct the eye to follow through to the seated background figure. This has to be a strong movement as each figure is contained in its own shape within the picture. This was an important aspect of the composition as the picture is about the isolation of the human figure. The curve of the bird's wing on the left of the picture is a movement to keep the eye contained in the shape. The spatial feeling is enhanced by the light tone of the foreground figure compared to the dark lost tones of the seated figure.

Choice of colour

The setting has the unreal quality of a stage set about it to give it a non-specific time and place setting. The colour is pervadingly warm, the figure in the foreground is warm in colour and tone compared to the background. To set about a picture of this nature, you need plenty of preparation. The size of the picture means that mistakes will be expensive in both time and

The body of the eagle.

The dark form of the eagle emerging.

energy. So, a number of preparatory drawings and paintings were necessary before embarking on such a large project.

Formulating an idea

If this is an aspect of picture making that interests you there are some things which you must be sure about before you start. With still lifes, landscapes or portraits your subject is there before you and there is a direct physical link between you, but once you move away from that situation then

Above and left: Sketchbook drawings for the torso, defining the main directional lines.

This painting was done from life in one short sitting of about two hours. The main purpose of this study was to gather information and also to build into the painting some of the qualities that I wanted in the final picture. The approach has been kept freer than in the large picture as this is still only a study.

there are other considerations. Firstly, and most importantly, is the idea. This is the foundation of your picture. If your idea is not sufficiently strong, then no matter how well you paint it, the painting will never stand up for long, in terms of the interest and intensity the spectator requires of a painting. Having satisfied yourself that the idea merits further development then your next requirement is to gather together more than enough information about the subject or content of the picture. This could be figures, architecture, landscape, atmosphere, or a combination of all these elements. When I say more than enough, it is necessary to be able to sieve through and discard what you don't need, rather than feel that you are scraping the barrel for information.

Painting the picture
When you have arrived at this point, then the process of painting the picture is almost the same as described for the previous projects in terms of composition, colour, shape, and line. The only

This is a sketchbook idea for parts of the larger painting, and was carried out to clarify my thoughts about the mood of the picture, rather than to make specific drawings about form and shape.

Below: This was one of many quick ideas for the painting in which colour was introduced into the sketches. These sketches are deliberately kept loose to allow for flexibility within the drawing and also to enable me to move quickly on to another sketch to develop ideas further.

difference is that this time you can do anything with your picture – you are completely in charge. It's rather like playing with plasticine (modelling clay), you can push and pull it into any shape you like, make spaces, close them off or change scale to suit your idea. It's a wonderful feeling to have this freedom in the creative process.

There are many painters who work in this vein. Graham Sutherland, one of the great English painters of the twentieth century, merits attention. The most interesting aspect of his work for us to consider is that a great deal of his work is landscape based but composed entirely in the studio. He used landscape, and took from it various aspects, changed them and set them back down in the landscape from which they had come. There is, however, an absolute authenticity about his work, due to direct observation. He changed, composed, and re-defined shapes, but they are always believable, and the considerations of composition and colour which you have been making throughout the projects and exercises in this section relate as much to his work as they will to yours.

To learn the rules and properties of oil painting is absolutely essential to you if you are to progress and develop your talent, and at the same time, liberate your creative spirit.

Graham Sutherland 'Horned Forms' 813 × 641mm (32 × 25¼in.). Sutherland is a painter who uses landscape rather than a painter of landscape. To use his own definition, he paraphrases landscape and forms which means that although his art is firmly based in landscape as his source of inspiration, he composes his pictures from various elements not necessarily from the same location. In this painting, one can see very definite landscape elements; the horizon line in the distance divides the sky and land mass, for example. The horned forms in the foreground have a menacing dramatic quality which, although their scale is large in the picture, probably came from quite small forms such as gorse thorns. This is essentially a picture composed of landscape and natural elements to express a particular personal feeling about an environment, and would have been arrived at through an acute personal observation using sketchbook studies and drawings.

181

PART FOUR

Composition
and
Perspective

Introduction

This vase from the fourth century BC is an example of the Greeks' use of perspective.

(Artist unknown) Japanese print 370 × 228mm (14½ × 9in.). None of the traditional Western methods of creating form by using tone or perspective has been used in this print. Emotion is expressed through the conflicting and powerful angles of the flat design.

Composition and perspective are powerful tools in artists' hands, once you have understood how to employ them. They are both concerned with the way that shapes and forms are ordered on the page and with creating works that make visual sense to the viewer and which have in–depth structure.

Composition is the organization of the shapes and forms into an expressive whole, whereas perspective produces the illusion of three dimensions on a two-dimensional surface. In most Western art the two work together, in a relationship that can perhaps be understood by an analogy with literature. In this, the role of perspective is like that of grammar, and composition like that of vocabulary. The compositional elements – line, shape, tone and colour – need to be ordered into coherent phrases and sentences, and this is the function of perspective – reproducing those elements in a form that can be 'read'. The roots of the two words also throw some light on their meaning. Composition derives from the Latin *compositus*, which means well-arranged, whereas perspective comes from a word concerned with looking – *perspicere*, to look through.

An artist, then, uses composition and perspective to present a coherent pictorial representation of elements of life and scenery from the world of our visual experience. Composition is present in any painting, from the moment you put two blobs of colour down next to each other, but perspective has only been conventional in painting from the late Middle Ages, and was to remain so until the early years of our own century. It is still a powerful tool in representational art. Simply put, perspective enables us to differentiate between forms of different sizes and at different distances from the viewer and to grasp immediately what those relationships are. Take a simple drawing by a child of two people against a background. The child will probably draw the two people in different sizes against some other objects, and it will not be possible to tell whether the smaller of the two is merely smaller than the other one, or is the same size, but is further away. Perspective enables you to establish such relationships in your work.

Although formal rules of perspective were not developed until the Renaissance, a simple form was known earlier. It was used by the Greeks in decorations on their pots and by the Romans in the mural paintings in their villas. But the Renaissance architects' use of space in their great buildings

challenged painters to find a means of equalling this concept of space on a two-dimensional surface, and this led to the great discoveries in perspective.

A study of perspective alone, however, does not make a work of art more (or less) beautiful. For centuries artists managed without it and more recently, since the experiments of the Cubists and the consequent development of abstraction, many artists have had no need for it. However, if you want to produce drawings and paintings that represent the visual world as you see it, a grasp of the principles of perspective will be invaluable.

The studies of composition and perspective are equally applicable, whether you are drawing or painting, but here the more direct approach will be studied through drawing. As in most disciplines knowledge and understanding give confidence, and in art this is as important as observation and sensitivity to form and colour. As you gain an improved understanding of these principles, you will find that your work will gain in confidence and that you will be better able to create a finished work from your sketches.

Valerie Thornton 'Cley Hall Farm' 400 × 572mm (15¾ × 22½in.). This sensitively balanced etching illustrates how depth is created without resorting to perspective in a composition in which the forms have been flattened, creating an almost abstract design. Depth is achieved by tone, and the scale of the textures. The carefully calculated lines on the left of the design are less intended to contribute to the feeling of depth than to give variation to the shapes created by the vertical and horizontal structure of the etching.

Many amateur artists and students fear that perspective is an abstruse subject, but in fact a grasp of the three-dimensional world is fundamental to our existence, and also to the mechanics of the eye and the way we perceive. It is a very straightforward process to gain a working understanding of the principles and to be able to use them to solve most visual problems concerning the size of shapes in distance. This section aims to teach the basic rules which will solve most problems, and at the same time to convey the principles of composition. It does this through giving a series of exercises, which are designed to be followed and put into practice. If they are read on the page without being tried out, they may sometimes appear to be complex and difficult, but if you actually do the drawings yourself, you should find that they are quite straightforward.

Another word of warning is to do them in sequence. They are designed to follow from one another, and if you skip or dip you may find that you are missing a vital piece of information that was given earlier.

Ultimately, however, your surest route to expressing the third dimension successfully in well-composed works is intense observation of your subject, careful study of angles and relative shapes and a feeling for space. Mastery of composition and perspective does not derive from learning a series of rules to which you have to adhere slavishly, but from the knowledge that gives the confidence to respond with spontaneity and excitement to the beauty of things you see around you.

'Hauled Out for a Polish'. This chalk study for a painting was done to establish the composition. The original view of the boats that I had was horizontal. From this study, however, I decided that a vertical shape was more appropriate for the purpose of the finished painting, which was to emphasize the unstable shape of boats out of the water.

Materials and equipment

A few simple tools will be needed to practice the exercises in this section: an A2 (594 × 420mm/ 24 × 18in.) or ½ Imperial (559 × 381mm/ 22 × 15in.) drawing board; A2 (594 × 420mm/ 24 × 18in.) white cartridge (drawing) paper; flat-headed drawing pins or masking tape for securing the corners of your paper to the board; a T-square to fit your drawing board; a 45° and 30°/ 60° set square (triangle), preferably of thick plastic and no less than 200mm (8in.) along the longest side – thin plastic bends and is liable to slip under a ruler or T-square; a pair of compasses for taking off measurements; H or F (2½-3) grade pencils – softer grades smudge easily; a 300mm (12in.) ruler – again, plastic is preferable to wood.

To use your instruments correctly requires no special skills. Hold your T-square arm hard up against the left side of your board to draw a horizontal line at any height across the board.

Slide the set square along the T-square, or along a firmly held ruler, or hold it underneath a horizontal line to locate the centre of vision and vanishing points of either a 45° or 30°/60° projection. The larger you make a perspective drawing with instruments, the easier you will find it to be accurate.

A useful hint when you are drawing a line to get it just where you want it is to put the point of a sharp pencil on the exact place you wish to start the line, slide your ruler, T- or set square up to it until it touches, then draw along. This is a great deal easier than trying to put the ruler in exactly the right point first.

Always keep your instruments clean, otherwise your drawing soon becomes dirty.

To prevent a plastic ruler or set square sliding about independently, stick a narrow strip of masking tape along the back.

You won't need a vast array of tools and equipment to practice the perspective exercises suggested: the most useful items are illustrated here.

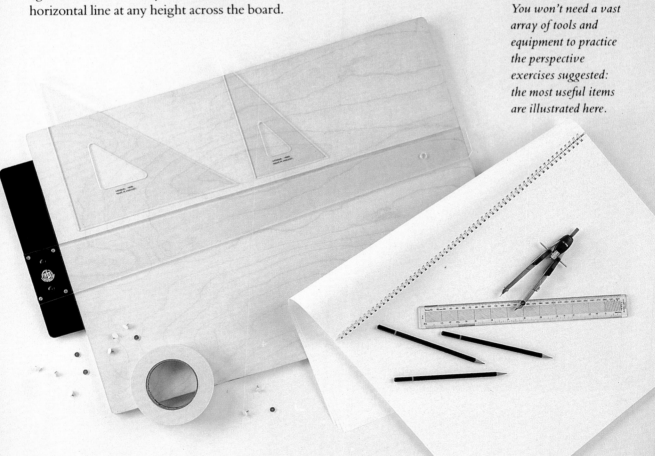

1 Composition

In his 'Notes on the Art of Painting' given to the Royal Academy in 1783 Sir Joshua Reynolds wrote:

'Composition, which is the principal part of the invention of a Painter, is by far the greatest difficulty he has to encounter. Every man that can paint at all, can execute individual parts; but to keep those parts in due subordination as relative to a whole, requires a comprehensive view of the art, that more strongly implies genius, than perhaps any other quality.'

In spite of Reynolds' rather pessimistic view, the principles of composition – arranging shapes within the picture area – once understood, can be mastered to good effect.

Sir Joshua Reynolds 'Self Portrait', painted 1753 or 1754.

The shape of the surface

For most artists the flat, two-dimensional surface is the stage on which they act out and convey all their emotional and intellectual ideas. Therefore, the size, shape and proportion of this surface have an important effect on a picture.

Artists' papers, boards and canvases are available in a very wide range of sizes and proportions and if you are making up your own canvases from stretchers there is an even greater choice of size. There is no objection either to cutting a board or piece of paper to the size and shape you would like it to be, so there is no need to feel inhibited by materials that come in stock sizes. You can work to any size and shape you feel comfortable with.

One of the most common shapes for easel paintings is the horizontal rectangle (diagram 1). Since its base is greater than its vertical sides, it produces a very stable shape. One feels it would be difficult to knock it over. The eye can roam

Diagram 1. The horizontal (or landscape) rectangle.

'Dangerous Reef' 485 × 700mm (19 × 27½in.). The powerful line of the horizon in this long composition is offset by the curves of the waves and the stern plates to exploit fully the overall shape.

Cosimo Tura 'The Virgin and Child Enthroned' 2390 × 1016mm (94¼ × 40in.). This painting shows Tura's mastery of design and creative use of perspective. He exploits the vertical format to the full, by repeating the arch at the top of the painting with the niche in which the Madonna sits, and underlining the height of the throne by the supporting figures and pillars on each side, which are emphasized by the two figures beneath.

Diagram 2. The vertical (or portrait) rectangle.

expansively from side to side and also back into the picture (this is termed 'recession'). This has been and still is a favourite shape of the English and Dutch landscape painters, among them John Constable, J.M.W. Turner, and Meyndert Hobbema; indeed it is known as 'landscape' shape in art circles. However, it does not invite the eye to travel up and down.

The same rectangle up-ended (diagram 2) presents a very different feeling. It is less stable and could be knocked over easily, the eye cannot move much from side to side and is inhibited from going deep into the shape. However, the eye can roam up and down. It can soar, and consequently this became the favourite shape of the great religious painters, like Botticelli, Crivelli, and Tura, whose subjects like the 'Assumption of the Virgin', or 'Christ in Majesty' or the 'Ascension' were perfectly conveyed by this format. It has also been the format of descents into Hell and a hilarious drawing of a Royal Academy soirée by Rowlandson of an avalanche of inebriated members and their ladies tumbling down the main staircase. It is not such an easy shape to fill as the landscape, but is ideal for portraits and has earned the name throughout the art world as 'portrait' shape.

The square (diagram 3) is the least evocative and most neutral shape, although it has great stability. It invites the viewer to look into its centre and the eye tends to roam in a spiral around that point. This tendency was exploited by the great

Venetian painters, Veronese and Tintoretto, the former in 'Unfaithfulness' from his 'Allegory of Love' series and the latter in 'The Origin of the Milky Way'. More recently, Pieter Mondrian used the square because of its neutral qualities and relied upon his sensitivity to shape and the space within it to overcome that inherent neutrality.

The diamond shape (diagram 4) has little equilibrium; it is just balanced and presents a challenge to the artist to create a balanced stable design within it. More complex variations of shape than even the diamond are being tried today, with artists assembling different shapes and sizes of canvases to produce very large paintings of dynamic and arresting designs.

The final shape we will look at is typical of a painting designed for an architectural setting (diagram 5). Its half-round, arched top cuts off the top corners of the rectangle, but artists frequently incorporate the surrounding architectural features outside the picture area as anchorages and fulcrums for the main directional lines when employing this shape.

Paolo Veronese 'Unfaithfulness' 1850 × 1850mm (74 × 74in.). In this brilliant example of the square format, vertical and horizontal lines through the centre of the picture intersect where the figure's hip joins her torso.

Diagram 3. The square.

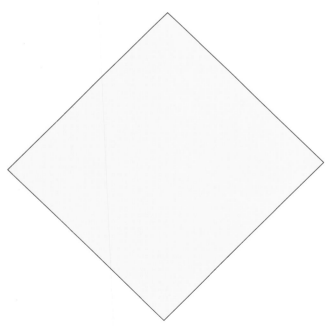

Diagram 4. The diamond.

Diagram 5. The arched rectangle.

Dividing the surface

The first impact that any work of art has upon the spectator is usually made by the arrangement of the main shapes on the surface and the divisions of the total space. Having considered which shape is most suitable for the idea you want to express, you need to think about how best to arrange or 'compose' your picture within the space. In any work the subject matter will be arranged in such a way as to impose some sort of basic division of the painting surface. What this is going to be is one of the first decisions to be made.

Taking a horizontal rectangle as the chosen shape (although many of the considerations that follow are equally applicable, whichever shape of surface you have chosen), the simplest division is by one line only. The most common way is a horizontal line right across the centre (as shown in diagram 6). This can be used by a skilful artist to good effect, but because each rectangle is equal, it is probably the least interesting of all arrangements. (Have a look at your own drawings and paintings and see if you have ever done this.)

The same rectangle, although still cut across by only one line as in diagram 7, is much more interesting when the two proportions are different. A division nearer the bottom of the painting gives you plenty of space for a fine sky or an interesting background. The foreground is reduced, so this division is ideal when the foreground presents you with several problems, since it allows you to cut out as much as possible.

The reverse of this (where the horizontal division is nearer the top of the painting, as shown in diagram 8), however, invites the artist to create an exciting foreground since it gives plenty of ground to cover to the horizon (assuming that you make the division coincide with the horizon). There is the opportunity to create a feeling of

Diagram 6. Divided by a central horizontal line.

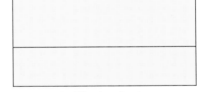

Diagram 7. The low horizon.

Jacob van Ruisdael 'Landscape with Ruins' 1075 × 1440mm (43 × 57½in.). Van Ruisdael was a master of composition. In this painting the low horizon gives room for the billowing clouds in the sky, which disappears beyond and below the horizon.

great recession, and for the interesting development of things near to.

Many artists content themselves with a simple horizontal division of their surface, but more often than not they will make a vertical division of their compositions as well. The most obvious division, into four rectangles (as shown in diagram 9), can be made to work in the hands of a great artist, but is very dull otherwise. This arrangement demands that something very exciting is put into each rectangle to make the whole work. This can be a handicap. However, a vertical and horizontal division producing a juxtaposition of rectangles (diagram 10) makes a more interesting framework for a composition.

Perhaps your decisions as an artist in composing your work have so far been intuitive and this is right, but why not review your work and see if these simple suggestions may help to give greater interest to your compositions?

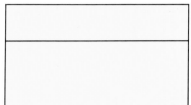

Diagram 8. The high horizon.

'Bathing Huts' 395 × 525mm (15½ × 21½in.). In this long composition the high horizon gives room for a full foreground. The study shows severe recession that takes the eye back in a rather lurching way into the design.

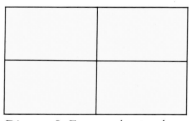

Diagram 9. Four equal rectangles.

'The Glebe Cottage' 405 × 550mm (16 × 22½in.). Here, the horizontal and repetitive lines of horizon, roof and walls are counterbalanced by the strong vertical through the chimney, gable and centre of the wall.

Diagram 10. Four
rectangles of different
sizes.

James McNeill Whistler 'Old Battersea
Bridge: Nocturne in Blue and Gold'
679 × 508mm (26¾ × 20in.). It is not
only to horizontal rectangles that the
considerations on dividing the picture
surface apply. In this upright painting,
Whistler uses the deliberately heightened
bridge to create the simple but dramatic
vertical and horizontal divisions and force
the eye upward to take in the firework
display. Although he is ostensibly
concerned with colour and tone to create the
atmosphere, he needed space for the display
on the right. He achieves this, and makes a
satisfying composition, through the four
unequal rectangles.

193

Harmonious proportion

Artists have always looked for both an ideal shape on which to work, and ideal proportions for that shape and several theories have evolved, two of which we will look at. The first is based on the relationship of squares and rectangles.

Construct a square ABCD (as shown in diagram 11). Produce the lines AB and DC. Using diagonal DB, describe an arc so that it intersects the produced line DC at F. From F draw a line at right angles to DF to intersect the produced line AB at E. The constructed rectangle AEFD has a harmonious relationship with the square ABCD. Repeat the procedure, using diagonal DE, to construct a further rectangle. This rectangle AHID has a harmonious relation with the square ABCD and the rectangle AEFD. This principle has long provided a rule-of-thumb method for artists seeking good proportion.

The second method of establishing fine proportion we will look at developed from the discovery of the Golden Mean, a direct result of the widespread interest in geometry and classical art in the Renaissance. The Golden Mean is also called the 'divine' proportion because while it is provable and demonstrable geometrically it cannot be resolved arithmetically, since it always results in an irrational fraction, .618 recurring.

Diagram 12 demonstrates how to discover the ideal proportion of a line AB (which could be the base or upright of a rectangle). Produce the line to C, so that CA is half the length of AB. From A draw a 90° vertical line AD the same length as AB. With the point of a pair of compasses at C describe an arc from D to intersect AB. The point of intersection G marks the Golden Mean of AB.

Diagram 13 is an extension of diagram 12. In it, the Golden Means of the rectangle ABCD are drawn in (in order not to make the diagram too unwieldy, the calculation lines of three sides, AB, BC, and CD only are shown). The points of intersection of the Golden Means W, X, Y and Z are also indicated.

It is interesting to look at how one of the great artists put the theory of the Golden Mean into practice. A study of the works of the English artist John Constable reveals that his paintings constructed and developed in the studio from studies made in the field always show his understanding of the Golden Mean. So familiar was he with this proportion that he used it instinctively when working on location and the knowledge never interfered with his spontaneity and freshness. His respect for the ideal or 'divine'

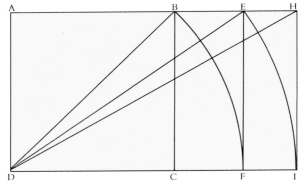

Diagram 11. The relationship of squares and rectangles.

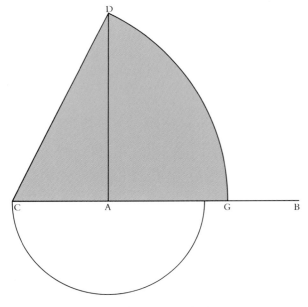

Diagram 12. The Golden Mean of a line AB.

194

proportion is evident from a detailed analysis of many of his works.

Constable regarded his painting 'The Cornfield', an upright design, as one of his best researched works, making studies beforehand of every detail, before building it into a fine satisfying painting. The parts did not appear in nature in the same positions as they do in the picture, since Constable has brought Dedham Church into view, in the background. The Golden Means have been calculated along with the main directional lines. It becomes very obvious that intersecting lines, whether within the main picture area or on the edges, assume a greater importance than disconnected lines which do not touch other lines or the edges of the picture. It is usually on these intersections that centres of interest are placed to great effect; those placed on the intersections of the Golden Means have the greatest effect. Try this exercise yourself with a reproduction of a great painting.

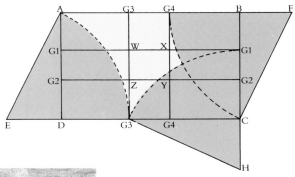

Above: Diagram 13. The Golden Means of a horizontal rectangle. These are found by taking each of the sides of the rectangle and determining its Golden Mean, as shown in diagram 12.

John Constable 'The Cornfield' 1429 × 1219mm (56¼ × 48in.). This painting shows Constable's understanding of the Golden Mean. The overlaid lines G1, G2, G3 and G4 mark the main Golden Sections, and it is along these lines that Constable placed his major points of interest, including the dog. The church, placed on an intersection of two of these lines has even greater prominence. The boy in the bottom left of the picture is exactly at the intersections of the Golden Sections of that rectangle: G5, G6, G7 and G8.

Creating a composition

Composition also involves arranging shapes within your picture area. Excited by a knowledge of proportion and shape it is tempting to be over-ambitious and use far too great a variety of shape within your composition. When three simple shapes, such as a triangle, rhomboid and circle, are placed separately in a composition or overlap each other (as shown in diagram 14), the viewer can identify each shape, read what it is and enjoy the interplay. The addition of one more shape, particularly an irregular one as shown in diagram 15, obscures their identities, however, and while the design may still hold up it would require only one more shape to create incoherence or confusion.

The last two points to consider here are, firstly, that a horizontal shape with easy flowing directional lines gives a sense of passivity or tranquillity, whereas strongly opposed lines and lines not parallel to the edges convey a sense of agitation, dynamism, or activity. Secondly, directional lines leading into corners take the viewer's eye out of the design. Avoid them unless you wish to create an impression of explosion.

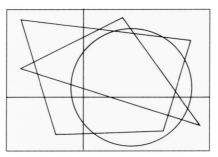

Diagram 14. Three shapes are readable.

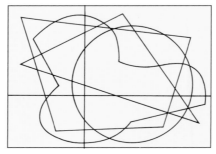

Diagram 15. One more is confusing.

PROVING MOUNTS (MATS)

Proving mounts are indispensable when designing a drawing or painting. Cut two L shapes from a piece of card (as shown in diagram 16). Gather all the work you have so far done, including those sketches you thought insignificant, and place the mounts around them. Then adjust the sizes and shape, taking pieces out of the picture, making square compositions long and upright from square. You may find, for instance, that instead of the horizon dividing your composition across the middle it looks much more interesting with less sky or even very little foreground.

Keep these proving mounts handy while composing your pictures – they will be of great assistance.

Viewing frames are also useful. Make three from dark-faced card – the first with a rectangular aperture of the proportions 3:5, based on the Golden Mean; the second with a square aperture

J.M.W. Turner 'The Evening Star' 900 × 1200mm (36 × 48in.). Although unfinished, this painting expresses a great sense of tranquillity. The equilibrium of the design creates a very still atmosphere.

Paolo Uccello ' Battle of San Romano' (detail) 1790 × 2950mm (71½ × 126in.). In this dynamic design, the *conflicting angles of the lances and juxtapositions of each feature lead the eye out of the canvas.*

3:3; and the third with a rectangular aperture of the proportions 3:4¼ based lengthwise on the diagonal of the square.

Practice is necessary to use viewing frames successfully; they can, however, be invaluable in helping you create a composition.

Close one eye and hold the frame a few centimetres from your open eye, then move it away until it is at arm's length. You will notice that the closer it is to the eye the greater the breadth of view you have through it, and the further away it is from your eye the narrower and more restricted is the view. Cut paper or prepare boards on which you are going to work to exactly the same proportions, for example, 30 × 50cm (12 × 20in.), 30 × 30cm (12 × 12in.) and 30 × 43cm (12 × 17in.). Find interesting still lifes or views from your window, and move your viewing frame until you see through the aperture how much you wish to draw. Then arrange the shapes as you see them through your viewing frame. (At this stage, work only in line. Don't try to add a third dimension.) Try moving your viewpoint lower or higher, and make drawings from these positions. Immediately your compositions will take on greater originality, and you will see shapes more clearly and use them more effectively than before.

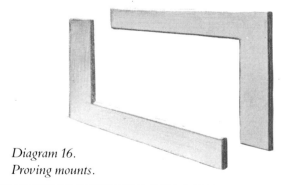

Diagram 16.
Proving mounts.

2 Approaching perspective

We have so far only looked at the linear aspect of composition, although we all know that gradations of tone of light to dark from white to black will add to the drama of fine composition. We are also aware, however, that we expect this flat composition – the two-dimensional structure of the surface – to be supported by an understandable structure in the third dimension. This can be achieved by tonal changes, by the use of colour or by an awareness of the principles of perspective. Perspective exists all around us – vanishing points, for example, can be traced from buildings and your eye level is a constant. Before we turn to the principles of perspective, and how they are applied in drawing and painting, however, it is necessary to become familiar with the technical terms that are used in dealing with perspective. These are not purely academic but have a practical value for the artist because they relate to and clarify the visual assumptions we make about the world around us.

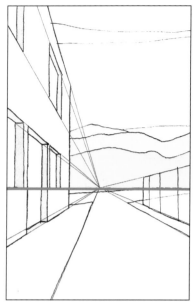

Diagram 17. In all diagrams, the blue line is the eye level.

Key terms

Almost everyone who has written about perspective, or who has taught it, has invented their own terms for the different elements. Some are widely used and well known, but others seem less familiar. To prevent confusion for those with some knowledge of perspective, and to establish these elements for those who are coming to it fresh, here is a list of the terms that I shall be using, together with definitions and alternatives you may meet elsewhere. The abbreviations are those used throughout the rest of this section.

Angle of Incidence The angle formed between a ray of light as it strikes an object and the object's surface.

Angle of Reflection The angle between a ray of light and the surface of an object as it bounces off that object. It equals the angle of incidence.

Centre of Vision – CV Also termed Central Vanishing Point (CVP), Point of Sight (PS), Principal Vanishing Point (PVP). This is the nearest point on the picture plane (see below) opposite your eye. It is found at the intersection of the lines of sight and eye level. Imagine that you are looking down the sights of a rifle held horizontally; the point of aim would be the centre of vision.

Elevation A drawing of what you would see if you were standing directly in front of the subject.

Eye – E (black bullet) Sometimes termed the Spectator (S) or Viewer (V). This is the point from which your eye views the subject.

Eye Level – EL (blue line) This is a complete horizontal circle at your eye level as you turn your head or the horizon if you are at sea level. Everything in perspective is related to this line.

Ground Line – GL A measuring line, this is a line running along the ground parallel to the eye level. A measured scale can be marked on it and projected back to the CV or VPs to give lateral measurements.

Ground Plane – GP An imaginary horizontal flat extension of the ground on which you stand, it extends forwards from your feet to the eye level on the picture plane.

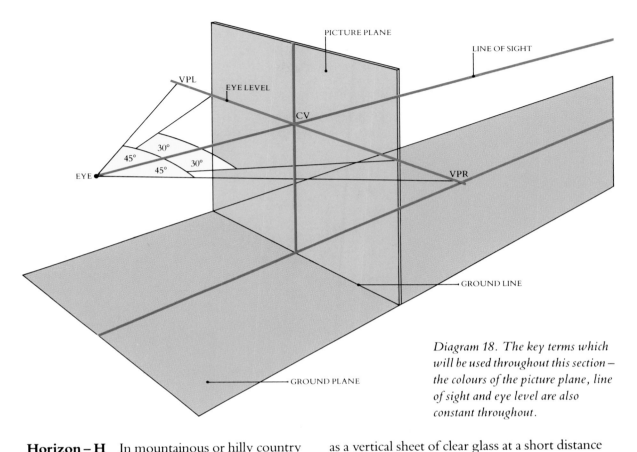

Diagram 18. The key terms which
will be used throughout this section –
the colours of the picture plane, line
of sight and eye level are also
constant throughout.

Horizon – H   In mountainous or hilly country it is the dividing line between sky and land and may be well above the eye level (or below in three-point perspective).

Line of Sight – LS (red lines)   Also termed Distance Line (DL). This is the line from the eye to the picture plane and which intersects it at 90°. Measuring it establishes the distance you are from the picture plane.

Parallels of Perspective   The term Vanishing Parallels (VP) is also used. These are lines seen on a plan as parallel, but in perspective they appear to converge at a point on the eye level at infinity.

Picture Plane – PP (solid blue)   This is an imaginary vertical plane at right angles to the line of sight upon which a drawing or painting is drafted. It can be regarded as the surface of your board or canvas. To help understand it, think of it

as a vertical sheet of clear glass at a short distance from you, through which you view your subject. What is seen on the picture plane is shaped by two factors: the height that the eye is from the ground line and the distance the subject is from the eye. The distance between eye and subject is usually equal to the greater dimension of your picture.

Plan   A drawing of something done as if you were looking at it from directly above.

Trace Lines   Lines which plot one point on a form to another, or the path of a shadow on an object on the ground plane or across the object.

Vanishing Points – VP   Also termed Distance Points (DP). These are points on the eye level on either side of the centre of vision to which parallel lines going away from you converge and appear to vanish. They can be extended to infinity to left and right – known as vanishing point left (VPL)

199

and vanishing point right (VPR). While for your subject the natural vanishing points may occur on or about the extremes of your board, it is likely that they may be some distance outside the edges. A piece of card pinned along the foot of the board can be fixed at an inclined angle, and two lines from a central point at the bottom drawn upwards in the approximate directions of the vanishing points as shown in diagram 19. This is a very inaccurate guide, but can be of use if you extend the lines in your imagination or point in the appropriate directions. You can persuade people looking at your work to stand back from the picture to the position from which you want it to be seen by placing your vanishing points further away from the edges of the painting.

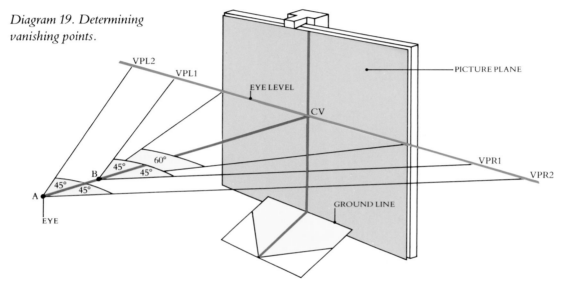

Diagram 19. Determining vanishing points.

How we see

Lines in a composition that slope inwards away from the edge of the picture immediately create the illusion of depth. In diagram 20 in real life the lines represented by AB and CD are assumed to be the same length, but AB appears further away than CD. On a similar assumption the points labelled E appear further away than F. This illusion is heightened by the line XY which we visually assume is a distant horizon. This diagram could be a drawing on a flat vertical wall.

In diagram 21 a similar visual assumption is made. AB appears much nearer than CD and EF. We tend to assume that each line is really the same height, and that the smaller ones are further away. This time XY leaves us in less doubt that it is a distant horizon. The three figures in diagram 22 are even more compelling in the way they assume their positions in space. We immediately think that figure C is nearest and A and B further away.

Let us now look at *how* these 'optical illusions' happen. Close one eye, then stand or sit upright

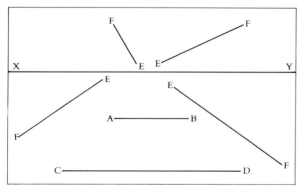

Diagram 20. We assume CD is nearer than AB.

and fix your gaze on a spot straight in front, level with your eye. Raise and extend both your arms and hands in front of you, then open your arms until you can no longer see your hands with any definition. Most people open their arms to about 60° before being unable to see the hands in clear focus, so the average 'cone of vision' is taken to be 60°. Perspective, in theory, does not work if both your eyes are open.

Imagine you are looking through a pane of glass at two identical vertical pegs in the ground outside as shown in diagram 23. The rays of light from the pegs converge on the eye. The rays from the one furthest away have converged much more than the nearer one so the further peg will appear smaller on the glass pane, and correspondingly the nearer peg will appear larger and below the one further away. Diagram 24 shows two lengths of timber lying on the ground first in plan view and then seen through a pane of glass. The lines of sight converging on the eye show the piece of timber GH appearing much shorter than EF where they pass through the glass.

Now imagine that the pane of glass you have been looking through is a piece of paper or board. The way in which your eyes have perceived the lengths of timber through the glass is the way you should draw them, measuring off their heights and lengths on to the paper.

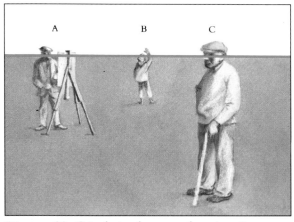

Diagram 22. C is obviously nearer than A or B.

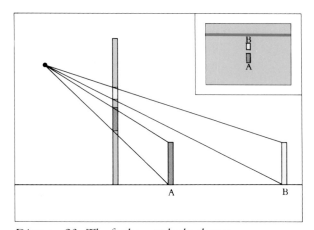

Diagram 23. The farther peg looks shorter.

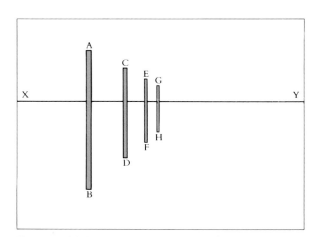

Diagram 21. We assume AB is nearer than CD.

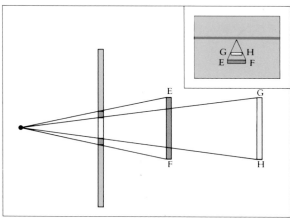

Diagram 24. The farther length looks shorter.

A classic example of these principles put into practice is the drawing of parallel railway lines disappearing into the distance (as shown in diagram 25). The tracks get smaller and closer together as they recede until the lines meet at a point on the horizon on the eye level – at infinity.

Left: Diagram 25. The tracks get smaller and closer together as they recede.

Aids to drawing

Over the years, artists, illustrators and draughtsmen have developed various ways to help them represent accurately what they see in front of them. These 'aids' to drawing, and you should remember that they are only that (not rules to follow slavishly or devices you must buy or make), vary from the simple and familiar to the more mechanical and technical. You may, however, find some of them very useful.

Measuring by eye with a pencil
A simple means of estimating and comparing proportions, particularly vertical and horizontal distances, is by using a pencil as a measure. Select the object you wish to use as a yardstick for your drawing, then hold your pencil out, making sure your arm is fully extended. Align the top of the pencil with the top of the object and your finger with the bottom (as shown in diagram 26). This 'measurement' will allow you to estimate the other objects in proportion. Ensure when

measuring depths that the pencil is absolutely vertical. When estimating pitch or measuring horizontally, the pencil has to be at right angles to your line of vision. When estimating an angle, start with the pencil horizontal, then rotate it until it lies along the line. This will establish the angle.

Sight size
Working 'sight size' is a useful technique to employ. Diagram 27 shows how this system would work when tackling a 'still life' of a cube on a small table. If you are right-handed, you will need to look round the left side of the drawing board so that your drawing hand does not cross the lines of sight and obscure your vision. With the board vertical and one eye closed, move your head slightly to left and right so that the board's edge can be used as a plumb line to determine the varying heights of each part of the objects, and mark these points on the edge of the board. This is particularly useful when figure drawing, but can also be used to good effect when drawing a landscape or, as here, a still life. This is a time-honoured method, proved by the ticks to be seen down the edge of many a master's drawing, indicating he was drawing sight size.

We perceive objects in a plane which is at right angles to our line of vision. In the case of looking straight ahead the plane is vertical, as if it were a sheet of glass suspended in front of us. However, when you are drawing your board may be on your knees or on a sloping easel, so that you will have to look down; the tendency, nevertheless, is still to

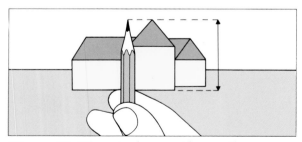

Diagram 26. Measuring by eye with a pencil.

visualize the vertical plane before your eye. To 'translate' this vertical image to a board at an angle requires complex mental adjustments of proportion. There is a danger that you may overadjust, making the bottom half of what you are drawing much too big. If you are a beginner, it is probably easier to use a vertical board until you have had more practice and are more proficient.

The obvious exception to using a vertical board is when drawing a horizontal subject, say a landscape-shaped still life or, indeed, a real landscape. It is then much easier to look over the top (as shown in diagram 28). Hold the board horizontally beneath your subject, but close up against it, with one eye closed. Then, with your free hand, tick off the widths of the details of your subject along the top edge of your paper.

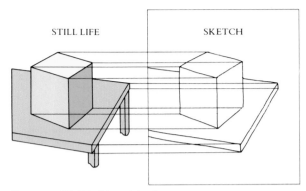

STILL LIFE   SKETCH

Diagram 27. Working sight size.

Your drawings might at first appear stilted or stiff using these methods; however, with practice the techniques will become instinctive and no longer inhibit your style.

Diagram 28. The principle of working sight size applied to a landscape.

Mechanical aids

Albrecht Dürer used a drawing frame with a rather elaborate mechanism. The eyepiece could be moved laterally with a thread and turnbuckle, and backwards or forwards, keeping it square with the table top. The glazed frame was also held vertically. A simpler version can be constructed with a picture frame, without its backing but with its glass, clamped on to a table. The critical part of this piece of equipment is the eyepiece. It must be steady for you to be able to produce accurate results. Position the frame and eyepiece so your arm and hand holding a brush loaded with permanent white gouache colour, or a chinagraph pencil (china marker), can reach the glass comfortably (this may take practice).

You will find that, as one eye is closed, it will, at first, be difficult to judge the distance your hand is from the glass. You then draw what you see on to the framed glass. Once the image has been completed, it can be traced off on to thin paper, giving you precise angles, shape and proportion for your drawing.

There are other mechanical aids to drawing, such as the Camera Obscura, which basically consists of a box with a magnifying lens. This produces an upside-down image on a screen which can then be traced off. A Camera Ottica is similar to a Camera Obscura but since it has a mirror inside, it rights the image produced by the lens; it does take some experimentation to make it work. Many eighteenth-century artists, including the great Venetian master Canaletto, are believed to have used such an instrument extensively. Such mechanical aids are fun to make and use, but are no real substitute for the judgements of your eye. Similarly a camera, although it can be a useful tool and reminder, and is to some people a source of inspiration, cannot give you the reasoned sensitivity to space that can be developed by keen observation and expressed by a sound understanding of perspective.

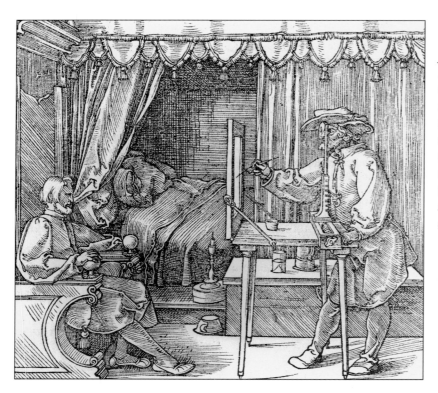

This illustration reproduced from Underweyssung der Messung, *first published in 1525, shows Albrecht Dürer's drawing frame in use. The artist moves the eyepiece back and forth until he can see through the glass as much or as little of his subject (here a figure) as he wishes to paint or draw. He can then trace the outline on to the glass. If he wants to paint a picture from this, he simply transfers the tracing on to his canvas.*

3 Principles of perspective

We now understand how converging rays make us see objects that we know to be the same size as varying sizes because of the different distances they are from the eye. The next step is to know how by applying the rules of perspective these variations can be expressed and appreciated in your drawings and paintings. You may find it useful to keep referring to the definitions of terms on pages 198–200, initially at least.

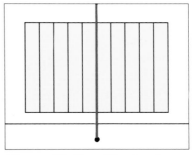

Diagram 29. Plan of floorboards.

Parallel perspective

Parallel perspective is employed when one side of what is facing you is parallel to the picture plane.

Take a plan view of floorboards, seen from above. As diagram 29 shows, they are all parallel and recede, and they are also all equal in width. When viewed on the picture plane, however (diagram 30), they converge and if extended meet at one point on the eye level which is at the viewer's centre of vision. As they are equal in width, their width measurements can be marked along the ground line at the foot of the picture plane. At any other point in their length the relative measurement of any board's width will be as it would be seen in perspective.

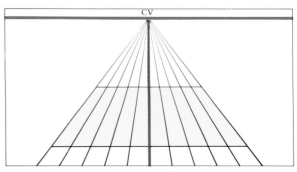

Diagram 30. On the PP, the boards converge.

The position of the viewer alters the appearance of the floorboards (as shown in diagrams 31 and 32). However, there is a limit as to how far you can move to right or left and still employ the rules of parallel perspective. As soon as you have to turn your head to see the whole object then you must use the rules of oblique perspective (see pages 213–16). At this stage we can summarize the first rules of parallel perspective:

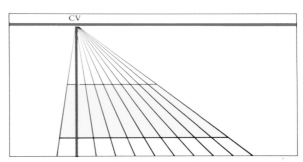

Diagram 31. View of boards to the right.

1 Parallel lines receding from the eye appear to converge and meet at a point at infinity. If these lines are in a horizontal plane and parallel to the line of sight, that point at which they meet is the centre of vision and is on the eye level.
2 Lines which are parallel to the picture plane, that is at right angles to the line of sight, have no vanishing point.

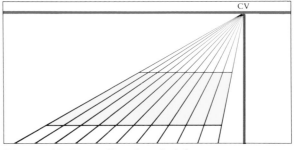

Diagram 32. View of boards to the left.

DRAWING AN INTERIOR

Having constructed a floor following the rules of parallel perspective, it is a very simple procedure to erect a vertical to any size you like at each corner and create an interior. Always start your drawings by establishing an eye level and a centre of vision. All the vanishing lines to the centre of vision are then fairly simple to plot.

The only new feature in the drawing below is the door ajar. Both the top and bottom of the door, since they are parallel, will vanish to a point on the eye level to the left of the CV. Once you have decided how far open you want the door to be, the vanishing lines of the top and the bottom can then be determined.

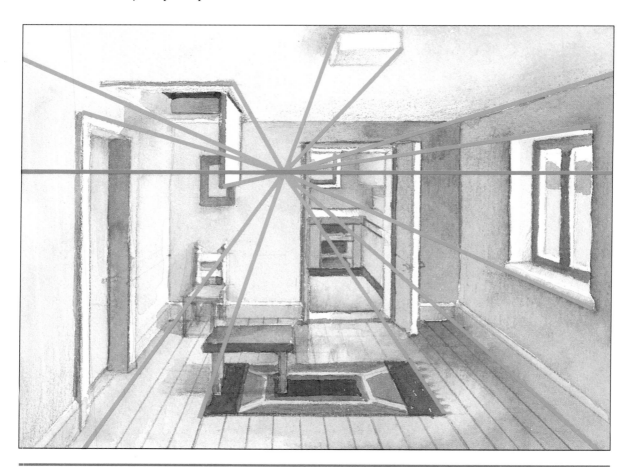

Using diagonals

It is useful to know how to find the centre of a rectangle or square whether in plan view or perspective. This is done by simply drawing in the diagonals. You will notice from the elevation of diagram 33 that the perspective centre makes the back half of square ABFE narrower than the front half EFCD. The diagonals of the square have their common vanishing point on the eye level outside the area of the picture plane. The real advantage of constructing these diagonals is that they allow you to measure the depth of each rectangle in

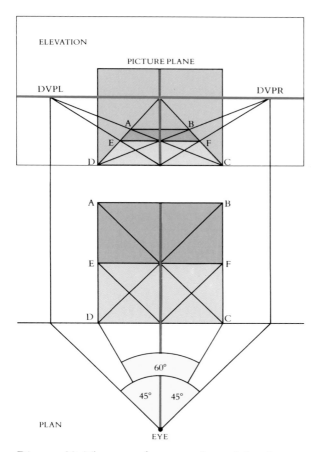

Diagram 33. The centre of a square, plan and elevation.

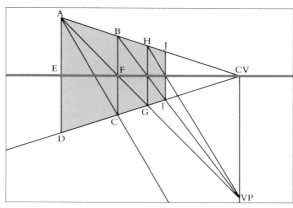

Diagram 34. Using diagonals to establish depth.

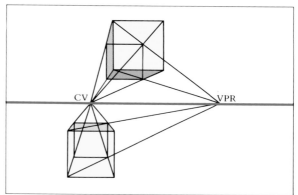

Diagram 35. Cubes above and below the eye level.

perspective, without resort to holding your pencil at arm's length, when you are drawing from objects or constructing forms from imagination or memory. In this way, you can achieve a convincing feeling of depth in your drawings and paintings.

It is not just horizontal distances that can be measured. It is also possible to measure the equal spaces between verticals in perspective (suppose, for example, you wanted to draw a receding row of vertical posts alongside a flat, straight road as in diagram 34). Decide where you want your first two posts to be. Then, establish a diagonal VP for the space between the posts, this will be immediately below the centre of vision. The diagonal AC produced will make a very long line

before it intersects a vertical dropped from the CV. Lack of space may make it impractical. A diagonal dropped through the eye level (E to CV), however, will work just as well. AF produced to meet a vertical dropped from the CV gives you your VP and the base of your third post (G). A vertical from G to H is your third post. A line from your VP to B gives the base of your fourth post (I) and so on.

Cubic shapes above and below the eye level can also be constructed by using diagonals (you may need the principles in order to put clouds in one of your pictures). A diagonal to the VPR in diagram 35 tells you where the back of the cube should be placed. The backs and faces are, obviously, drawn in parallel perspective.

A SIMPLE COMPOSITION

You should now be able to make very interesting drawings using simple parallel perspective and diagonal parallels. Establish your eye level, then decide compositionally what you want to appear facing you (here the ends of the buildings). Draw those in (here, since all the roofs are parallel, their slopes are also parallel). Diagonals are used here to establish the spacing of the fence posts on the right, although they too recede to the CV. The fence posts on the left are parallel to the PP, so don't recede.

Calculating depth

The calculation of depth (that is, where the 'back' of the room should be placed, or how far away the next fence post should be) of a shape in perspective initially seems a problem. If you are working on sight, you can measure it with your eye, or if in doubt with a vertically held pencil. If you can confine the shape you are drawing in a square or rectangle, the diagonal vanishing points can be fixed and depths established in that way. A simple way when working in the studio or to gain

a clear understanding is to make a plan as in diagram 36. This shows how a shape ABCD behind the picture plane and ground line can be accurately placed. The lines of sight intersecting the picture plane establish the widths of the back of the shape. When the width of the back is dropped vertically on to the vanishing parallels, you can establish the precise depth of the square.

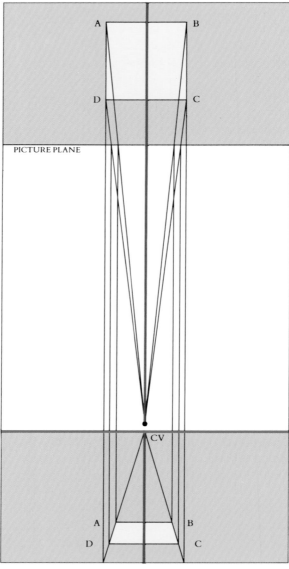

Diagram 36. A plan to enable you to calculate depth.

Placing figures in a landscape

A common problem is to depict people scattered on a flat surface and to establish their relative sizes. Draw a measuring line vertically on the left side of your board. In diagram 37, our artist standing with his sketch pad is 1.8m (6ft) tall and the other seated artist is 1.1m (3ft 6in.) high. These two measurements are projected back to the centre of vision and they represent a 1.8m (6ft) and 1.1m (3ft 6in.) height from the ground for the whole depth of the drawing. By carrying horizontals to left or right the whole area is covered by these measurements. The figures are placed between those lines where they compositionally fit.

A more common problem, and one over which students and experienced artists stumble, is how to place a figure or an object accurately in front of the picture plane (without making it appear that they are standing in a trench or on a chair).

Diagram 38 illustrates what we see with a normal eye level at 1.5m (5ft) from the ground. This is fixed by a measuring line, once again up the left-hand side of the picture plane. This time the receding lines on the ground have been extended forward of the picture plane as well as back to the centre of vision. From this, it is clear how much of the figures in front of the picture plane should logically be included in the composition.

Diagram 37. Relative heights of figures in a landscape.

Diagram 38. Placing figures in front of the picture plane.

Inclined and declined planes

Many artists have used inclines and declines in their compositions to create an almost giddy feeling of recession in their designs. The principles involved in creating inclines and declines are the same as those used with a flat horizontal plane with the exception that if the vanishing points are parallel to the horizontal plane, they will appear immediately above or below the centre of vision on which parallel receding lines will converge.

Normally you would not have to calculate the angle of slope but would rely on the sureness of your eye viewing the subject. However, in a composition in the studio, the angle may well

'Holiday Chalet'. An example of inclined planes.

have as much to do with your compositional need for a line going in that direction as the precise angle of slope.

Diagram 39 shows three shapes A, B and C. All are the same width, and in parallel perspective all would recede to the CV. However, if you wanted A to slope downwards and C to slope up, you have to establish vanishing points immediately above and below the CV. The descending slope from A to D in this diagram from the position of the decline vanishing point (VPD) shows how little of this plane would be seen.

Slopes can be established by incline and decline VPs. In diagram 40, the straight road first runs level (A) then slopes down (section B). The vanishing point for the decline (VPD) is indicated. The road then runs level again (section C). This section vanishes at the CV. The road then ascends gently (section D) and the vanishing point for the incline (VPI) is indicated. Finally the road levels off and disappears to the centre of vision at the eye

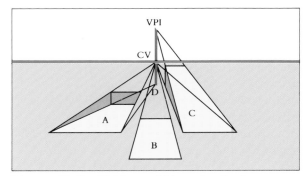

Diagram 39. Establishing vanishing points for slopes.

level. The fencing and wall slope at the same angle as the road, and because they are parallel to it, their vanishing points coincide.

Roofs, of course, are inclined planes and where they appear in recession (roofs A, C and D in diagram 41), they will have an incline vanishing point above the CV. The slopes of roofs B and E will not have vanishing points as they are parallel to the ground line and picture plane.

'Northern Suburb' 375 × 612mm (15 × 24½in.). Receding roofs create a convincing feeling of space.

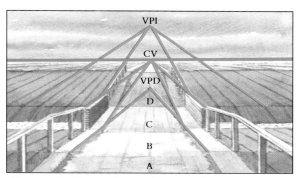

Diagram 40. How to draw a sloping road.

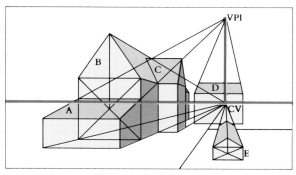

Diagram 41. Establishing VPs for roofs.

A STREET SCENE

You now have almost all the knowledge you need in order to be able to create a design with a descending and ascending road in recession, lined by buildings. There are two further points to understand.

Firstly, houses nearly always appear to go down in steps. Secondly, roofs, doors, windowsills and lintels are usually horizontal and so vanish to the CV, not the VPD. Establish your eye level and centre of vision, then decide how much of a decline you want in your street. Decide on a decline vanishing point, immediately below the CV. The tops and bottoms of the houses on the slope will vanish to the VPD.

Drawing circles and ellipses

We know that circles fit into squares and from diagram 33 we know how to draw a square in perspective. Circles or ellipses always have to be constructed in parallel perspective. Diagram 42 shows how ellipses can be constructed. Draw a square in perspective, and draw in the diagonals. Draw the front half of a circle from A to B freehand, touching C. Lines to the CV through where the half circle crosses the diagonals will give you the points through which to draw the back half of the circle.

There is one important point to remember if you are using this knowledge of ellipses to draw cylinders. You will remember from diagram 33 that the perspective centre of a square made the front half look bigger than the back. This is also, obviously, true of the centre line of an ellipse – it will make the back look smaller than the front. For this reason, you do not find the width of a cylinder by dropping verticals from the extremities of the perspective centre line, but from the widest portion of the ellipse. This is shown in diagram 43. The contours or edges that you would see are the lines XY and WZ.

When you are drawing cylindrical objects, it is better at the start to draw the whole ellipse, although only a portion of it may be seen. In this way the smooth rhythm of a compressed circle is best obtained. When you are satisfied with your shapes, erase those lines you don't need.

Once you have mastered drawing ellipses, all sorts of round and curved items – bicycles, pots, cups and glasses – can be included with effect in your compositions.

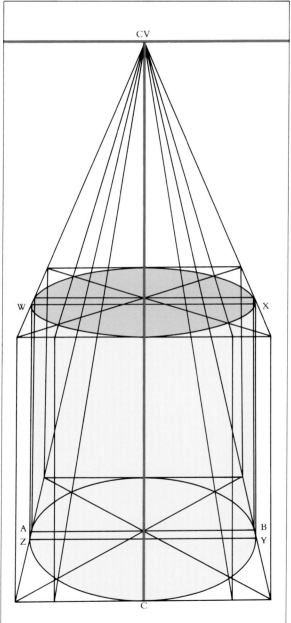

Diagram 43. Drawing a cylinder.

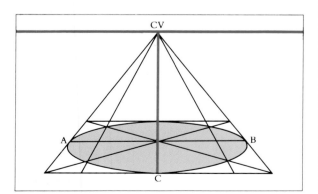

Diagram 42. Drawing a circle in perspective.

Oblique perspective

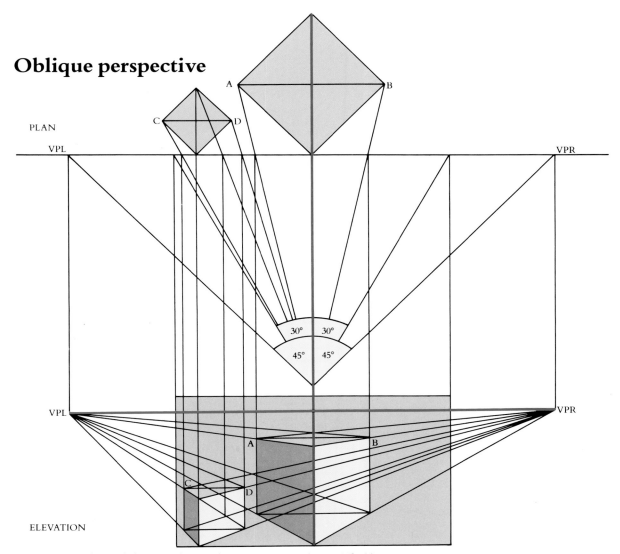

Diagram 44. Plan and elevation showing how to construct cubes in 45° oblique perspective.

A moment's observation reveals that objects in nature rarely oblige by lying parallel and at right angles to the eye level. They are nearly always at angles to it. Rules of perspective still govern these random dispositions, however, and, when applied, they help artists to create convincing form and space, and make a forceful contribution to composing a picture.

We have seen (pages 206-8) that by creating a 45° angle on either side of the line of vision vanishing points can be located that are in fact the points to which diagonals of squares in the design

converge. This gives a geometrically calculated and convincing depth. Vanishing points are not necessarily at this 45° angle from the line of sight, but perspective (rather like some games) works well if you make rules from convenient assumptions. A useful set of rules can also be assumed if a 60°/30° perspective is used. They again will allow you to establish relative depths coherently and yet they will produce a totally different viewpoint and appearance.

Diagram 44 is similar to diagram 36 on page 208. It shows a 45° perspective from a top plan projection and an elevation. It is very unusual for a creative artist to use a projection like this and I wouldn't recommend that you do either, but it does help you to understand how the lengths of the sides of the two squares are seen on the picture plane by the lines of sight passing through it, to the eye. These sizes projected down to the elevation form the basis for constructing the cubes. The size of the picture is governed by the 60° cone of vision.

One important point to notice is that where the edges of the squares are parallel to the vanishing parallels, the diagonals of each square AB and CD are parallel to the picture plane, that is, they are horizontal. The second point to notice is that the closer you get to the edges of the 60° field of

vision, the more distorted the cube appears. Outside that field of vision objects become progressively more distorted as the smaller cube illustrates. This looks more like a rectangular attaché case than a cube (to have avoided drawing it like this, you would have to have been standing further away). Perspective, then, has its limitations. As an artist, you must understand and either compensate for, or decide to exploit, these limitations.

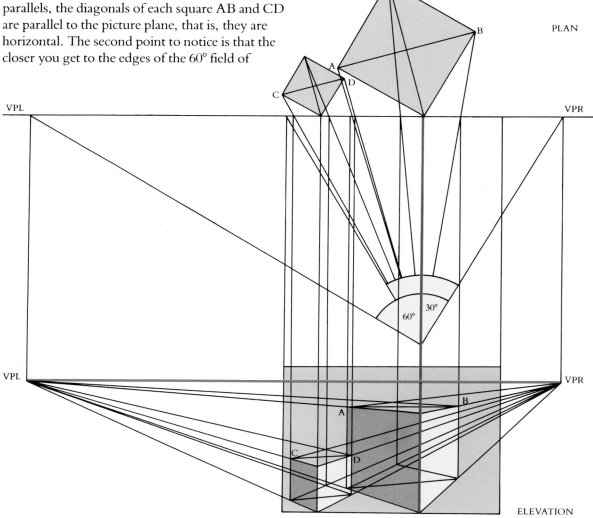

Diagram 45. The same cubes in 60°/30° perspective.

Diagram 45 demonstrates what happens to these cubes in 60°/30° perspective. The differences are obvious. Firstly, far more of the near side of the cubes is visible. Secondly, the vanishing parallels are again parallel to the sides of the squares, but these are more oblique to the eye level and picture plane than they were in 45° perspective. Also, the distortion of the smaller cube does not look so great due to the greater distance it is from the VPL. Finally, you can see that the diagonals of the cubes are not parallel to the picture plane or to eye level.

Diagrams 46 and 47 show these points in a 'real' situation. The first uses a high eye level and is drawn in 45° perspective. We are viewing the buildings from a distance, so no distortion occurs.

Gable ends and fronts are equally seen. In the second, although the centre of vision is in almost the same place, the buildings are angled at 60°/30°. Their structure is still right-angled but because of the acute angle of vision we can see the front more fully and the gable ends less so. The gap between the buildings has also disappeared and the sharper angles give a less symmetrical look to the group than in the 45° perspective drawing.

Depth in oblique perspective

As we saw in the section on parallel perspective, ascertaining convincing depths in perspective, at first, seems difficult. There are many ways of doing this (as discussed on pages 206–8), and here ways to establish depth in oblique perspective are shown. The square WXYZ in diagram 48 has been constructed in 45° perspective, its depth established by the diagonal XZ. The diamond-shaped square ABCD is simply put into WXYZ, its diagonal corresponding with the perspective centre of WXYZ and parallel to the eye level.

Occasionally, however, you will want to establish the depth of a square that is less conveniently angled to your line of sight and eye level. The square ABCD in diagram 49 is more typical of the kind of problem you will find! Draw WXYZ in as a guide. From points A and C, draw lines parallel to the sides of the square XY and WZ, then draw in the diagonal of WXYZ (ZX).

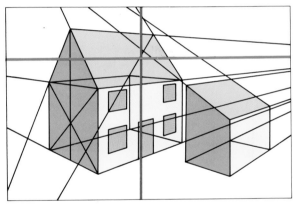

Diagram 46. View of houses in 45° oblique perspective.

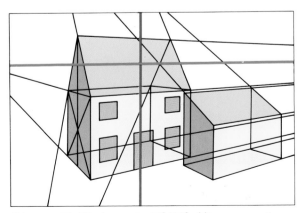

Diagram 47. The houses in 60°/30° oblique perspective.

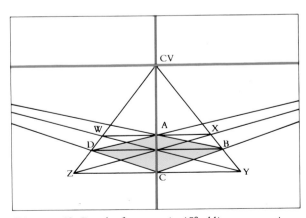

Diagram 48. Depth of a square in 45° oblique perspective.

From the points where these lines AE and CF intersect the diagonal (G and H) draw horizontals to WZ and XY to create the small interior squares FXBG and DHEZ. This can now be drafted into WXYZ which in diagram 50 has been constructed in parallel perspective. The lines EA and CF (measured along the foot of square WXYZ) recede. From the intersection of EA and CF with the diagonal XZ, the position of D and B can be ascertained. The square ABCD can then be constructed. DA and CB converge and if produced can be checked for accuracy. They meet on the eye level at VP.

This knowledge of oblique perspective should now enable you to create an interesting composition. Always decide first on an eye level

and place your vanishing points and centre of vision where you wish them to be. A simple rule of thumb if you wish to be accurate is, when using 45° perspective, to make your vanishing points equal distances from the centre of vision. The further apart you place them, the further away you are from your picture plane. If you are using 30°/60° perspective, the 60° vanishing point is roughly three times further from the centre of vision than the 30° vanishing point is. Although this is not a strictly accurate figure, it is a reasonable working estimate, and if you apply it you will find that it will generally produce convincing drawings.

Inclines and declines

Inclined and declined planes were discussed on pages 209–10. A knowledge of oblique perspective, however, enables a more convincing use of inclines and declines. Diagram 51 illustrates the way they could appear in a small harbour. Since this is in 45° oblique perspective, the right and left vanishing points are equal distances from the centre of vision on each side. The VPs are a long way outside the picture plane to left and right, indicating that the artist was standing well back. Also, because this is a sea view, the eye level is also the horizon. The ramps or hards incline and decline and their vanishing points lie immediately above and below the right-hand VP.

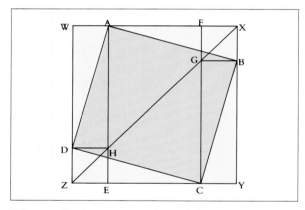

Diagram 49. An inconveniently angled square.

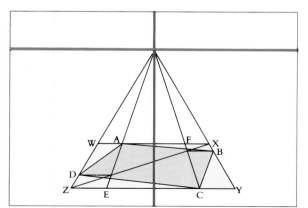

Diagram 50. The same square in plan view.

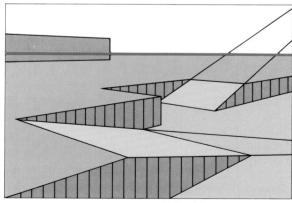

Diagram 51. Inclines and declines in oblique perspective.

A KITCHEN SCENE

This illustration is a very simplified version of the corner of a kitchen projected in 30°/60° perspective, and you now have all the knowledge you need in order to draw something like this. As already stated it was necessary to establish the eye level, the centre of vision and the 30° vanishing point on the left and the 60° vanishing point to the right. Such drawings can be put together even away from the subject without difficulty, if each point is established and logically constructed.

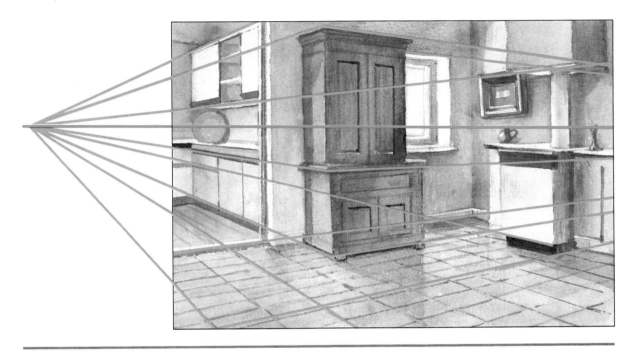

'Dinghies on the Hard' 473 × 640mm (19 × 25½in.). The almost random ridges along the inclined slopes – formed by planks being set on the still wet concrete – contribute to a powerful impression of recession. The boats, under covers, create a lateral rocking rhythm, but do not cut the composition in two because the lines of the foreground extend upwards to the top of the picture through the masts.

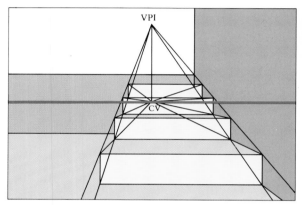

Diagram 52. *Stairs in parallel perspective from the side.*

Stairs

The perspective of stairs and of steps, rather like that of the roofs of buildings, is based on the presence of inclined and declined planes. Diagram 52 shows a series of stairs seen from the side and in parallel perspective. The lines connecting the treads (AB and CD) are parallel to EF and GH, although due to the recession of the stair treads,

'Mortlake Steps' 398 × 440mm (16 × 17½in.). Here, bank, causeway, wall and steps all contribute to recession.

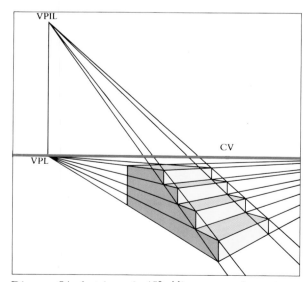

Diagram 53. *Stairs, seen from in front.*

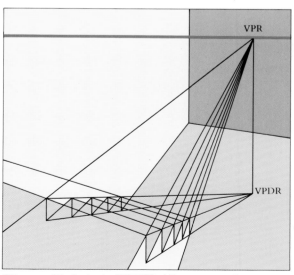

Diagram 55. *Stairs in 30°/60° oblique perspective.*

Diagram 54. *A staircase in 45° oblique perspective.*

EF and GH are much closer than AB and CD. In stairs viewed from the front and in parallel perspective, however, these tread lines all converge on the VPI (incline), which is immediately above the CV (diagram 53).

In a staircase seen in 45° oblique perspective (diagram 54), the tread lines converge on the VPI left which is immediately above the VP left. As in diagram 52, the lines connecting the front treads are farther apart than those connecting the rear.

Normally, we view stairs in very sharp perspective when we are about to go down them, as we are not only looking straight down from above, but have the added height of our own bodies. The visual effect of this is shown clearly in the 30°/60° projection of diagram 55.

AN ARRANGEMENT OF STAIRS

A complex and fanciful arrangement of stairs, like this one, should now be within your capabilities. These are in a 30°/60° projection. Establish your eye level, and decide where you want the stairs to come into your drawing. Next decide on the height of your stairs. Indicate the slopes of the stairs by deciding on the VPI and VPD. Constructing the arrangement should not now present you with any problems if you follow the preceding principles.

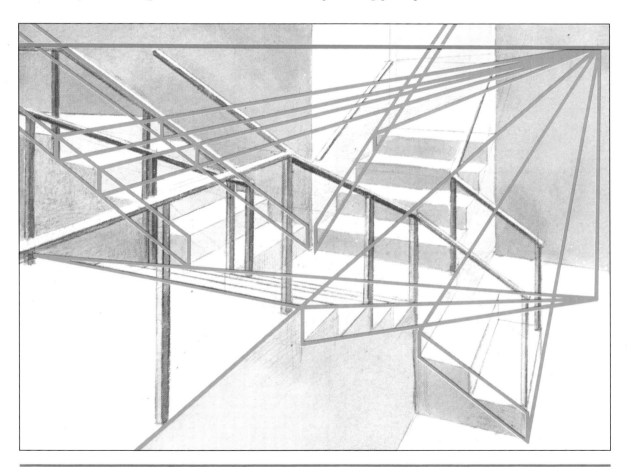

4 Shadows

When you are drawing or painting objectively, shadows cannot be ignored. They make shapes which are compositionally as important and as interesting as the objects from which they are cast (sometimes more so). They can often clarify the shapes and forms of these objects, which may otherwise be ill defined. They can also compel the artist to create tonal pattern, which must be co-ordinated with the other design elements to make an effective contribution to the emotional or descriptive content of the picture.

At various periods in the history of art, shadows have been employed to produce a romantic effect called 'chiaroscuro' (meaning light and shade), which enabled the artist to make some features of his design clear and distinct while others were shaded in gloom. This created a sense of mystery. Rembrandt was one of the great masters of this technique, and although the light and dark passages in his paintings defy perspective logic, they are totally convincing.

Sunlight usually gives better defined shadows over the whole of the picture plane than artificial light and the sun's shadows have a logic which can be seen as incorrect by any viewer if it is ignored. It takes masterful handling (composing) to use such light and shadow creatively and correctly.

'Fleet Sunset' 369 × 419mm (14¾ × 16¾in.). The recession along the beach is here reinforced by the diminishing scale of the mooring posts. Not only do the posts give the feeling of distance, they also help to explain the relative sizes of the boats.

220

Sunlight shadows

The size and extent of shadows produced by sunlight depend on the position of the sun in relation to the artist and the picture plane, on the time of day, and on the shape of the objects illuminated. An important point to remember about shadows produced by sunlight is that they are continually moving. After a few hours' work in front of a subject in sunlight, you will find that the position and size of the shadows have altered considerably. A few quick notes in a sketchbook from time to time will enable you to decide later where they are most appropriate compositionally.

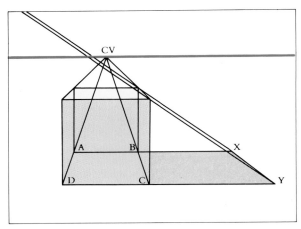

Diagram 56. Shadows of a cube in parallel perspective.

Rays parallel to the picture plane

Shadows cast by the sun's rays falling on an object in parallel perspective on to a level surface are also parallel. The sun's rays in diagram 56 are parallel to the picture plane and the sun is on the left. The length of the shadows is determined by the point at which the sun's rays intersect the lines AB and DC extended along the ground plane, at X and Y.

This applies to any object in parallel perspective. Diagram 57 shows a cylinder. Again, the sun's rays can be traced on the ground plane from lines parallel to the picture plane. In this case, the length of the shadows is determined by the distance from the cylinder's edge, hence the elliptical shape to the end of the shadow. This diagram also shows how the shadow reinforces the description of the shape upon which the sun's rays are falling.

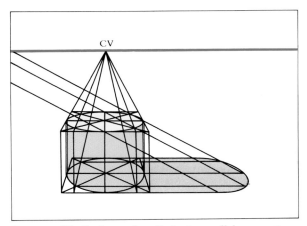

Diagram 57. Shadows of a cylinder in parallel perspective.

This is demonstrated more forcefully in diagram 58 in which a cube has been turned through 45° and projected in oblique perspective. The sun's rays, which are again on the left-hand side and parallel to the picture plane, determine the length and shape of the shadow by their intersection with lines drawn from A, B and C parallel to the ground line. The shape of the shadow explains the form and angle of the cube.

As we have said, obviously the time of day and to some extent the season in which you are working influence the length of the shadows that

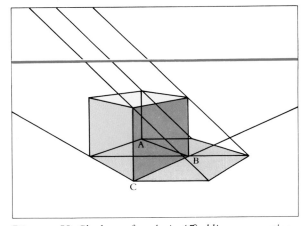

Diagram 58. Shadows of a cube in 45° oblique perspective.

will be cast. In winter, sunlight produces long shadows; a high noonday sun, however, produces very short shadows.

Shadows cast on an inclined slope are longer than those cast on a declined slope. In diagrams 59 and 60, the sun's rays are parallel to the picture plane. To find the length of the shadow on an incline (a pitched roof, for example), first find the horizontal plane. Extend lines from the CV through C and D to the edge of the roof and then around and down the sides of the building until they reach the horizontal line XY (parallel to the eye level). Extend the sides of the chimney AD and BC downwards until they reach the horizontal plane. Extend lines from points W and Z back to the CV; where they intersect AD extended to E, and BC extended to F gives you the forward plane of the shadow. Extend EF to G (drawn back also to the CV) and parallel to the ground plane. G is the point of intersection of the sun's rays, and the bottom extent of the shadow.

Shadows on declined planes are simpler. Extend DC up the slope, parallel to the angle of the roof, until it is intersected by a sun's ray from B at E. Trace from E back to the centre of vision. A line from A to the line ECV gives point F. Then, trace the far side of the chimney up the incline to F. This gives you the length and width of the shadow.

Sun immediately above the CV

Different phenomena occur when the sun is immediately above the centre of vision. In diagram 61, the sides of the shadow on the ground plane appear to incline inwards and when extended meet at the centre vision on the eye level. If, on the other hand, you were looking down on this cube, you would see the sides of the shadow, in fact, as parallel.

Diagram 62 demonstrates what happens to a wall with doorway and window when the sun is immediately above the CV, seen from directly in front. The sides of the shadow converge along the ground plane to the centre of vision.

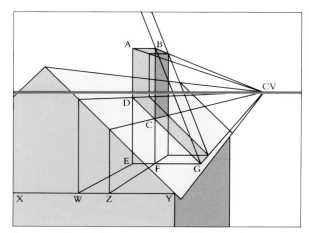

Diagram 59. Shadows on an inclined slope or plane.

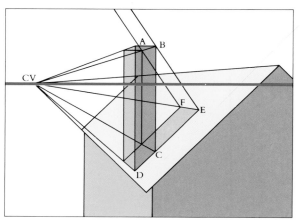

Diagram 60. Shadows on a declined slope or plane.

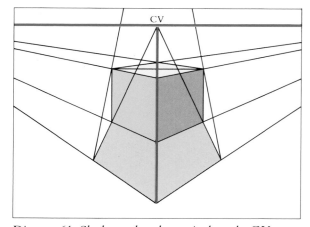

Diagram 61. Shadows when the sun is above the CV.

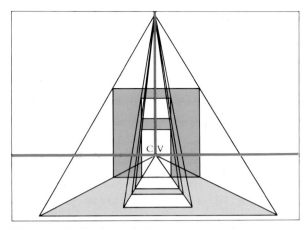

Diagram 62. Shadows of a doorway and window.

Sun to the left or right

Since the sun moves continually, you can't rely on it being directly to your left or right (and parallel to the picture plane) or straight above you. You will often have to cope with it in other situations and may in any case choose, compositionally, to place it elsewhere. In diagram 63, the sun is in front and to the artist's left. What is interesting now is that the vanishing point for the shadow

(VPS) is on the eye level and immediately beneath the sun. It would stay immediately beneath the sun even if the ground sloped. If it sloped upwards, the VP would be above the eye level; if it sloped downwards, the VP would be below the eye level, but in both cases, directly beneath the sun. Because the prism is drawn in oblique perspective, its vanishing points are out to the left and right of the diagram on the eye level.

Diagram 64 demonstrates how you would calculate the length and shape of a shadow if the sun were behind your left shoulder, just opposite to where it was in diagram 63. In this case you have to assume a position of the sun below the eye level; this will allow you to place the vanishing point of the shadow on the eye level. The assumed position of the sun should be as far below the EL as the sun really was above and as far to the right of the CV as the sun was to the left. Rays from the assumed sun to the top of the prism intersect with lines back from the base of the prism to the VPS. This determines the length and shape of the shadow. The vanishing points for the prism are on the eye level outside the diagram area.

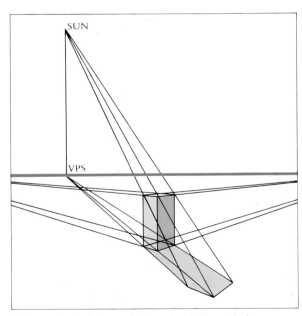

Diagram 63. The VPS is immediately beneath the sun.

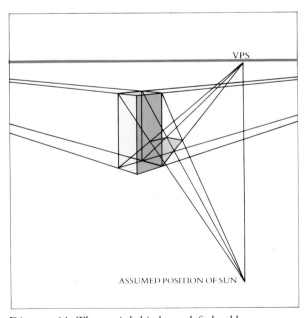

Diagram 64. The sun is behind your left shoulder.

Still with the sun behind your left shoulder, diagram 65 shows what happens to our wall pierced by a window and a door and its shadow. Again, to give the appearance of the sun being behind your left shoulder, the assumed position of the sun is the same distance from the centre of vision to the right as the real sun is to the left.

Assuming that you are on flat ground, then the sun must be the same distance below the eye level as the real one would appear above. The vanishing point for the shadow is directly above the assumed sun's position on the eye level. The length of the shadows is determined by rays from the sun to the various points of the wall intersecting the vanishing lines to the VPS (shadow).

Shadows of a building with a sloping roof and chimney are illustrated in diagram 66. The chimney's shadow is cast on the sloping roof and on to the level ground. The shadow of the chimney on the roof has a vanishing point as far above the eye level as the vanishing point for the incline but immediately below the sun at VPS1. The vanishing point for the shadows on the ground plane (annotated VPS2) is on the eye level, directly beneath the sun. The length of the chimney's cast shadow was calculated by taking the trace lines of the chimney down to the ground plane and then back to VPS2. Trace lines were then drawn to the right until intersected by the sun's rays at A. It is interesting to note that the shadow of the chimney on the inclined slope of the roof does not appear immediately above the one on the ground plane. You have to calculate each one separately. The drawing is in 45° oblique perspective.

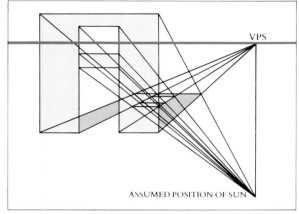

Diagram 65. Again, sun is behind your left shoulder.

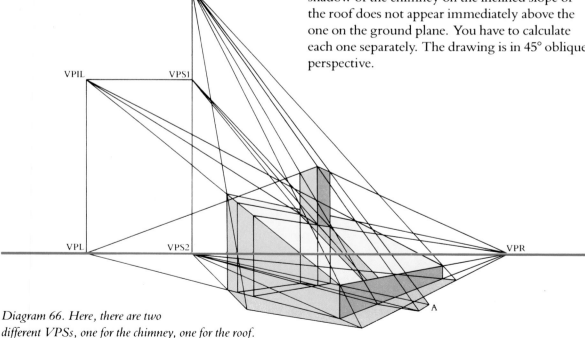

Diagram 66. Here, there are two different VPSs, one for the chimney, one for the roof.

Artificial light

Shadows cast by artificial light radiate from a point immediately below the light itself. These shadows, although well defined when near to, and in the main direction of, the light, become diffused as they get further away. They also are more distorted than shadows cast by sunlight.

Shadows produced by artificial light (the source of the light is indicated in these diagrams as ALS) have vanishing points immediately beneath the light and on the same plane as the objects which cast the shadow. This gives two radiating shadows.

Diagram 67 shows a cylinder. The extent of its shadow is determined by the intersection of the light rays and the vanishing point. The curved top of the cylinder can be determined either from points on the arc, or from diagonals of the square into which it fits (see page 212).

When the objects that cast the shadow are higher than the light source, the vanishing point of the shadow, obviously, is immediately above the light source.

Very often what we see is illuminated from more than one light source, so shadows form improbable shapes and, where they overlap, varied tones. Diagram 68 illustrates how that occurs. The vanishing points for the shadows are immediately below each of the two light sources. The trace and extent of the shadows is determined by the intersection of the light rays and the VPSs. The edges of the shadows appear much softer than those caused by direct light. Also, you will find two distinct tonal values in the area of shadow. The outer, lighter shadow is known as the penumbra and the darker central area of shadow as the umbra. The larger the light source, the smaller the umbra.

You will find a similar effect with a large or long source of light such as a tube light or even (if it is not in direct sunlight) a window with daylight passing through it. Because the light rays are emitted from the whole length of the source, you

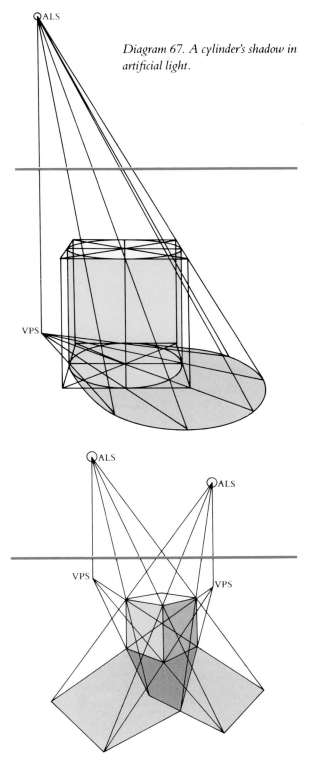

Diagram 67. A cylinder's shadow in artificial light.

Diagram 68. The cube illuminated from two sources.

225

get what may, at first sight, appear to be a confused shadow. For practical purposes, in a case like this, to construct the shadow take light rays from the centre of the tube or window and each end. Consequently you will have three vanishing points on the plane on which the object stands, immediately beneath each source point.

A ROOM IN SHADOW

This drawing with furniture reduced to fairly basic shapes shows the shadows produced by artificial light in a common situation. To draw a room like the one illustrated here, a vanishing point for shadows has to be established on each plane. The first is on the ground plane immediately below the light, and a second is on the chimney breast at the same height as the light. This establishes the shadows cast from the picture and fire surround. The third is level with the light but on the alcove wall, and is used to establish the depths of shadow from the shelving. A fourth, above the door, fixes the length of shadows from the pictures and chest of drawers on the wall facing you. A fifth would be on the far right wall outside the picture plane. This has to be plotted in order to give the length of shadow beneath the curtain. The radiation of shadow, which is the result of one central light source, is very typical of indoor artificial lighting.

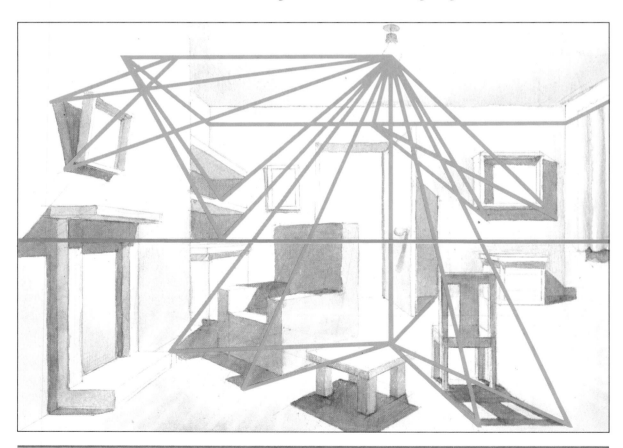

5 Reflections

To many artists the word reflection suggests water. There are, however, many other surfaces that reflect to a greater or lesser degree. The very best reflecting surface is mercury or mirror, but polished metal, a glazed picture or window, some plastics and even gloss-painted surfaces will give interesting reflections. Wet slates will reflect chimneys and wet pavements, figures and lampposts, lights and anything else on them. Sand along the shore, when wet, also gives a reflection. Often these surfaces are not level and slope at angles, which can complicate the reflection, but once the principles are understood the reflected shapes are not difficult to determine.

Agitated water reproduces images at improbable angles, the concavities actually reflecting objects the right way up, while swirls of lines cross, recross or zigzag across the surface. Surfaces are sometimes classified as producing regular and irregular reflections, but it is often difficult to know how to differentiate. Here, we will discuss flat water as a reflecting surface but rippled water is a large and complex subject. One of the major attractions of water that is near is that it reflects less light and, because it is transparent when clear, the bottom becomes visible (if you are in deep water, it takes on the hue of the ocean). The further away you view the reflection the clearer it appears. Vertical objects appear better defined, whereas horizontal ones may not seem to be reflected at all. Lights (such as the moon) on still water give a constant width reflection.

'Low Tide' 232 × 345mm (9¼ × 13¾in.). This chalk drawing on pale blue paper was done quickly on the quayside at Looe in Cornwall. The very shallow water reflects the warehouses and the high harbour wall.

Reflections in water

Most of the examples given here are illustrated in relation to boats, since they are more often associated with water than any other objects.

An object reflected in water is seen as far below the surface as it is in reality above. The reflecting ray to the eye cuts the surface and produces an angle (the angle of reflection, R) which is equal to the angle made from the point on the surface to the object (the angle of incidence, I). This principle governs all reflections, no matter what size the objects are or how far away they are. This is shown in diagram 69.

The reflecting surface is not necessarily the eye level, or even the horizon at sea. Diagram 70 shows a navigation mark, which extends exactly the same distance below the reflecting surface as it is above. More solid objects (a mooring post, for example) can create reflections whose sides appear to be of a different length. In diagram 71, for example, A and B are clearly the same length, but C and D appear different. They are not. They appear so because the angles of recession, extended, converge on the eye level at the centre of vision. An object which is not parallel to the

picture plane, however (like the length of timber in diagram 72) does have a reflection that is a different length from the object. The reflecting surface is projected forward from the CV to a point vertically below the nearest end of the timber (where a pebble dropped from C would strike the water at E); D is exactly the same distance below the surface. Both the object's and its reflection's lines of direction when extended will, if produced far enough, converge at a point immediately above and below the centre of vision and equidistant from it.

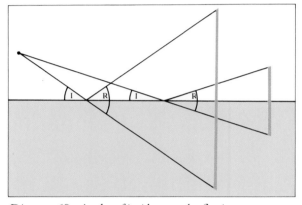

Diagram 69. Angles of incidence and reflection.

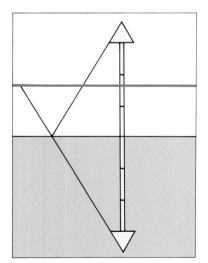

Diagram 70. The reflection is the same depth as the mark.

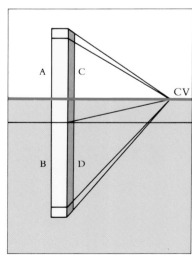

Diagram 71. The reflection appears longer, although it is not.

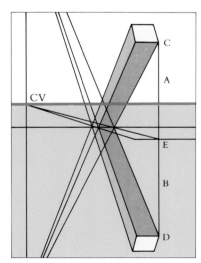

Diagram 72. The reflection is a different length from the object.

Diagram 73 illustrates a very common phenomenon of a flagstaff on the stern of a motorboat. The top of the staff is precisely the same distance above the reflecting surface as its reflection is below. This has to include the height of the stern of the boat. Note how the lines of recession converge on the centre of vision. The reflection of the stern shows a much steeper angle than the object itself because it is in parallel perspective. The same principles apply to buildings on a riverbank or at the seashore. Diagram 74 illustrates equal sized buildings at different distances from a riverbank and their reflections. A piece of the bank has been cut into like a dock to show how this works. Each vertical has to be brought down to the reflecting surface and then continued just as far below as it is above – this includes the height of the bank. Had we not

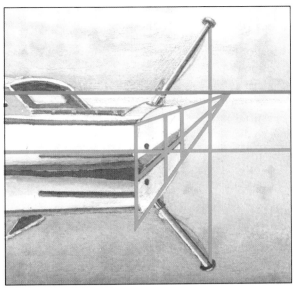

Diagram 73. The reflection of a flagstaff in water.

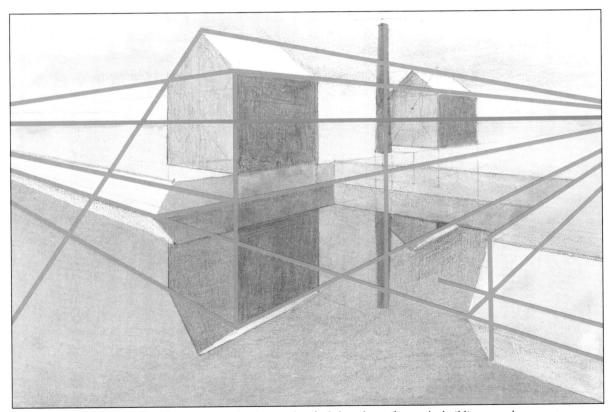

Diagram 74. Reflections of buildings on a riverbank extend as far below the surface as the buildings are above.

cut away the little dock all that would have been reflected of the rear building would have been the tip of its chimney. Note how the reflection of a sloping bank is ascertained by again taking back the level of the reflecting surface until it is vertically beneath the top of the slope. This is then extended the same distance downwards and the points connected.

The reflections of bridges show more of the underside of the constructions than does the direct view. Diagram 75 is projected in parallel perspective, so all the lines vanish to the same point. Those below the reflecting surface are the same distance from it as those above. A bridge in oblique perspective (diagram 76) has vanishing points outside the picture plane. For this reason,

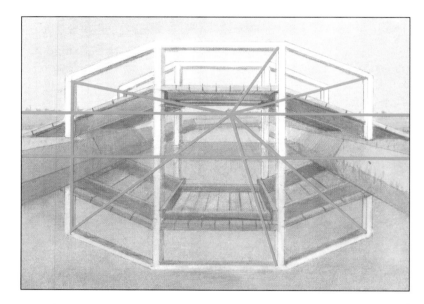

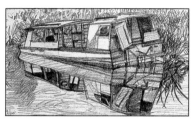

'Derelict Houseboat' 310 × 455mm (12½ × 18¼in.). This study for a painting gave many compositional opportunities to create improbable shapes from the derelict boat and its reflection in the river.

Diagram 75. In parallel perspective, all the lines vanish to the same point.

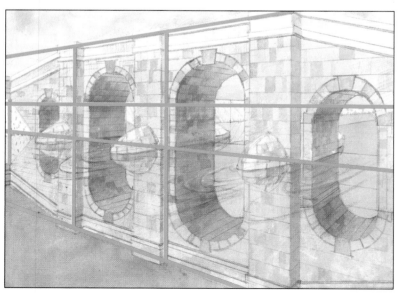

Diagram 76. In both parallel (above left) and oblique perspective (left), more of the underside of the bridges than the direct view is visible.

we can see through the arches. Each arch was constructed from a half square in perspective (see page 212). From then on, the construction is the same as for the bridge in parallel perspective.

Reflections on a wet surface – the reflection of a chimney on a sloping wet roof, for example – give shapes rather like shadows. The area of the reflection is determined in the same way as described in diagram 59. The only difference is that the reflecting surface slopes at an angle and the object is vertical. The easiest way to cope with this is to turn your drawing on its side and visualize the reflecting surface as being level, with the chimney tilting.

When the eye level is below the roof, it is still easier to turn your drawing on its side.

Reflections in glass

Reflections in a mirror are rather like looking through a hole in the wall into another room. The halfway marks between objects and their reflections occur on the mirror wall. Once you have established these marks, use a pair of compasses to describe an arc from the object to its reflection. In parallel perspective, everything slides across from the room into the looking glass. Don't forget, though, that objects will be laterally inverted: the position of the door knob changes, and you see the front of the chairback in the room and its back in the reflection. Remember too that in this situation the angles at which pictures tilt will be reversed.

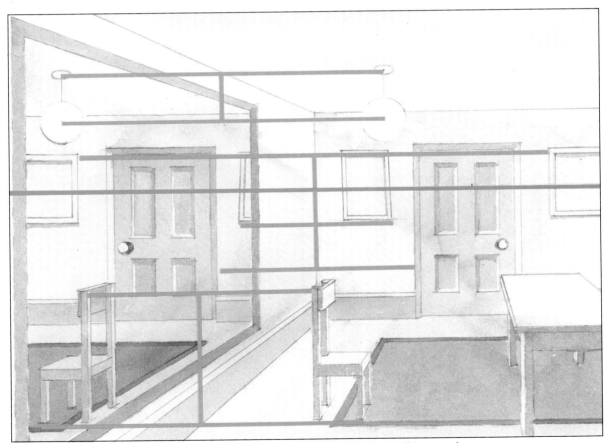

Diagram 77. Reflections in a mirror are rather like looking through a hole in a wall into another room.

6 Composition in practice

It is impossible to place a line on a piece of paper without attempting to draw it in the right place. All pictures have a compositional element. They have in common a sense of the third dimension and are strengthened by the feeling that the design and drawing go on behind the picture plane.

One of the most emotive elements of composition can be the planes which direct our eyes back into, up and across the picture. For this reason, planes are well worth establishing very early in your design, in fact second only to the horizontal and vertical arrangement of shapes and other main movements within the design and the shape you consider best communicates what you have to say.

Your picture's unity (which includes the shapes, tones and colours you use) is indissolubly linked to what you have to say. Remember that it is better to say one thing strongly and unequivocally than to try to say many things. That approach can make the painting fussy, splintered and without unity. Even a painting of a single object needs composing so that the very character and essence of the object are distilled in every shape. Consider your viewpoint, try sitting low on the floor or ground, look at your subject through undergrowth or the back of a chair. Climb high, sit on a table and look down upon your subject. See it in full light with the sun or a window behind you, or stand your subject directly in front of the light. Each position will have something of interest, so choose what, to you, is most exciting and best communicates your intentions. Make sketches, then detailed studies from nature and finally reconstruct the experience into a composition, when all your knowledge and skills of perspective and composition can be brought into play.

The advice and illustrations that follow will help you to employ your knowledge of perspective to create satisfying and meaningful pictures. However, the finest study of composition is to look closely at your favourite paintings by great masters. Trace the designs, find the Golden Sections, then the proportion of the rectangle, then the linear structure. Determine the eye level and principal vanishing points by tracing back the lines of recession, then look at the tonal shapes and masses. These studies will demonstrate that there are as many ways of composing as there are artists: the suggestions given here should not be seen as rules but as guidelines.

Ken Howard 'Saskia, Morning Light' 600 × 500mm (24 × 20in.). This masterly painting is held together by a well-considered geometric design. Although light is as much the subject of the painting as the model, there is a well-conceived spatial relationship between the two- and three-dimensional aspects of the picture. It is interesting to note that the vertical division of the composition is broken by the bent legs of the model, giving excitement to the painting. Note too how the areas of greatest highlights are juxtaposed against the darkest tones and perfectly balanced. There is also a subsidiary linear rhythm of light lines. The light shining on the model's chemise is echoed on the bottle on the table in the foreground and adds a further highlight to the painting.

Creating space

You have probably used, and must certainly have seen works by artists who use, the device illustrated in diagram 78 – putting one object in front of another – to create a feeling of space. By overlapping these shapes a sense of recession is created. This can, however, be ambiguous: you may just be putting a series of inverted 'L' shapes together. To give the impression of putting flat squares one in front of the other, another element is needed. Employing simple parallel perspective in the design, however, leaves no doubt which form is in front of the other and what that form is. Although cubic shapes are used in diagram 79, the principle can easily be applied to a sky filled with great cumulus clouds one in front of another, for example.

Symmetry and balance

Total symmetry and balance, although a common compositional ploy, need not be shunned. Many great pieces of architecture are designed symmetrically and it was used extensively in the fifteenth and sixteenth centuries for paintings of crucifixions, annunciations and other religious subjects. In diagram 80, the fulcrum (F) locates what we know instinctively as the centre of interest. This is a very convenient point around which to compose and on which to centre the action of a painting. It may be at the centre of vision or fulcrum of a mechanically structured design, or at the intersection of the important dividing lines of the painting (see pages 191-3). Many ploys can be used to assemble the directions and forms to direct attention to this spot. There

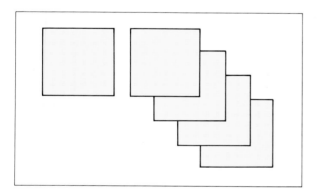

Diagram 78. Overlapping helps to create recession.

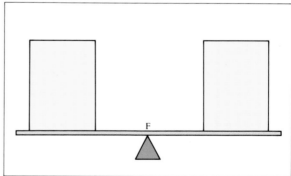

Diagram 80. A completely symmetrical arrangement.

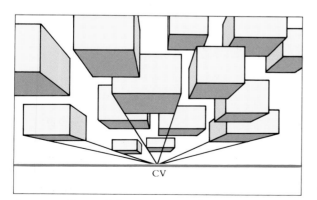

Diagram 79. Parallel perspective reinforces it.

Diagram 81. How to use the arrangement above.

may be possibly very little of importance at that point, it could just be a pinion, or it may be the most interesting point of the picture.

In diagram 81, the fulcrum, the centre of vision and centre of interest are focused at this one point.

Diagram 82 shows an alternative way of achieving equilibrium. The greater mass has the shorter arm of leverage, and the smaller form has the longer arm. This ensures that they remain in balance. In a composition based on this framework (diagram 83), the centre of interest is at the fulcrum and the most compelling centre of interest of all is employed, one of figures.

However small a figure is in a composition, it commands greater attention than more inanimate and elaborate forms. If you link a figure with the fulcrum and/or centre of vision, the eye gravitates straight to it.

In diagram 84, the centre of interest is again at the centre of vision and fulcrum. The mass nearest the fulcrum is hanging below the horizon and is a satisfactory balance to the object above it.

These masses can be made to balance by not necessarily being of greater or smaller area but by being of light or dark tone, or of subdued or vivid colour, or of intense subject interest and detail.

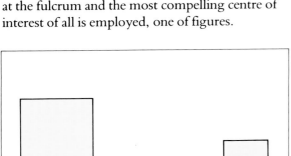

Diagram 82. A different way to achieve balance.

Diagram 83. How to use the arrangement on the left.

Diagram 84. Here, the centre of interest is at the centre of vision and fulcrum, but the larger mass (the boat) is below the horizon and balances the smaller mass above the horizon.

Achieving movement

There are many interesting possibilities in giving a painting or drawing movement. In a static piece of work actual movement is out of the question, but skilful use of shapes, repeated with progressively slight variations, will bounce the eye around a composition. Spots of similar colour or tone placed at intervals over the surface of a painting will cause the eye to move from one to the other, and lines, whether real or simply divisions between one tone and another, can compel the eye to move around wherever you wish.

Tone

Distance affects the tonal values of objects, as well as their colours. Before the nineteenth century, painters made distant passages of their work progressively more blue, without understanding the atmospheric changes that made this appear correct. If there were no atmospheric interference with light rays, black rocks, for example, would look black, and snow peaks white. Now we know that the very light and most reflective areas at a distance – snow-capped mountains, for instance – are not modified by the weaker, short-waved ultra-violet colours, so leave the red and infra-red long waves to penetrate the atmosphere. Thus, snow peaks look pink. The very darkest areas which reflect little or no light will appear at a distance lighter than they really are, so that black rocks will look blue. This is because the diffused ultra-violet short waves reach the dark areas, making them look blue or blue-violet. Half-toned colours depend upon the circumstances of light at the moment. If comparatively dark they will appear lighter, if fairly light they may seem warmer and darker.

'Work Boat' 512 × 705mm (20½ × 28¼in.). This study in gouache was composed on location. I chose the viewpoint that I felt showed the character of the boat to best advantage.

Index

Note: Page numbers in italic refer to illustrations

A
acrylic primer 141, 142; *142*
'alla prima' 136, 160
angle of incidence 198, 228; *228*
angle of reflection 198, 228; *228*
Artists' colour 132; *132*

B
Baldwin, Martin *130*
bamboo pens 20; *60*
blotting 90, 104, 122; *104*
blowing 102,112; *102, 113*
body colour *see* gouache
Botticelli, Sandro 189
box easels 23; *22*
brushes 21, 79, 84, 87, 92, 93, 100, 106, 124, 134-5, 146, 169; *79, 84, 135, 146*

C
camera obscura and ottica 204
cameras 204
Canaletto, Giovanni 204
canvas 138, 140; *139*
canvas boards 142; *138*
carrying straps 172
cartridge (drawing) paper 20, 142; *138, 142*
centre of vision (central vanishing point, point of sight, principal vanishing point) 198; *199-200*
charcoal 20
    charcoal drawing 44-6; *44-7*
    using charcoal 40, 44; *40*
charcoal pencils 20; *58*
'chiaroscuro' 220
circles and ellipses 212; *212*
coatings *see* glue size
colour 88, 89, 92, 94, 95, 96, 97, 108, 110, 121, 123, 125, 155, 157, 160, 162, 163, 165, 166, 167, 177; *117, 118, 157, 164, 165, 166*
    mixing 81, 85, 92, 149, 150; *85, 149, 150*
    wheel 148; *148*
composition 77, 95, 110, 112, 123, 124, 162-4, 168, 176-8, 181, 184, 188-97, 232-6; *95, 117, 119, 168, 188-97, 233-7*

see also preliminary sketches
compressed charcoal 20
cones of vision 201
Constable, John 152, 171, 189, 194-5; *170, 195*
Conté, N. J. 20
contrast 94, 95, 96, 97, 113, 122; *113, 119*
Cotman, John Sell 86
cracking (crazing) 169
craft knives 21
Crivelli 189
Cubists 185
curves, drawing 29; *28*

D
dabbing off 104; *104*
Daler board 142; *138*
dark 101, 111, 113, 123, 124, 125; *113, 123, 125*
Degas 50
depth, calculation of 208; *208*
details 92, 96, 97, 98, 113; *97, 98, 99*
diagonals, use of 206-7; *207*
diluents 136
dippers (palette cups) 137
directional lines 177, 196; *178*
doodles 153; *153*
dragged paint brush techniques 152; *152*
drawing aids 202-4; *202-4*
drawing boards 21, 82, 84
drawing positions 23-4; *23, 24*
dry brush 77, 104, 105; *104, 118*
drying 102, 130, 132, 133, 136, 137, 172; *91, 102*
Dürer, Albrecht 204; *204*

E
earth colours 132, 133
easels 23, 82, 137; *22, 82, 86*
elevation 198
emulsion (latex) primer 141, 142; *142*
enlarging 37; *37*
erasers 21, 40, 46; *47, 61*
eye (spectator, viewer) 198; *199*
eye level 163-4, 198; *198-200*
eyes (tonal range) 38; *38*

F
figures in landscapes 69, 209; *69, 209*
filberts 134; *134*

fixatives 21
flowers 122, 125; *114, 119, 122, 125, 143*
focal point 112
format 37; *37*
fountain pens 21
fulcrums 234, 235; *234, 235*
furniture 23; *22*

G
Gaa, Christa 117; *117*
Gainsborough, Thomas 72
gardens 115; *114, 117*
glazing 150-1, 169; *151, 169*
gloss 136
glue resist 55; *55*
glue sizes (coatings) 140
Gogh, Vincent van 16; *17*
Golden Mean 194-5; *194-5*
gouache (body colour) 80, 83, 117, 129; *73, 117*
gouache resist 54; *54*
Gould, Cheryl *143*
ground line 198; *199, 200*
ground plane 198; *199*
grounds 141, 160

H
hardboard (Masonite) 141; *139, 142*
highlights 158-9, 165; *159*
Hobbema, Meyndert 189
Hockney, David 86
horizons 191-3, 199 (defined); *191-2*
Howard, Ken 232; *7, 8, 160, 170, 233*

I
'impasto' 129
inclined and declined planes 209-10; *209-10*
ink 21
    working with ink 41; *41*
interiors, drawing 206; *206*
intersecting lines 195; *195*

J
Jones, Olwen 117; *119*

L
landscape 72, 108, 115, 122, 123, 124, 171-4; *108, 172, 173*
landscape rectangles 188-9; *188*

Acknowledgements

Swallow Publishing wish to thank the following
people and organizations for their help in preparing
Art Class. We apologise to anyone we may have
omitted to mention.

Unless indicated otherwise, all artwork is by the
authors of the respective sections of this book: Jason
Bowyer, Charles Bartlett, Roy Rodgers, and
T. W. Ward.

Martin Baldwin, p. 130; Stephen Bitti, p. 148; The
British Library, p. 204; The British Museum, pp. 17,
50; Christa Gaa, p. 117 (foot); Ken Howard, pp. 7,
8, 150, 170, 233; Olwen Jones, pp. 107, 119; The
Provost and Fellows of Eton College, Windsor, p. 73
(top); By kind permission of the Henry Moore
Foundation, p.53; Reproduced by courtesy of the
Trustees, the National Gallery, London, pp. 189,
190, 191, 195, 196, 197; The National Portrait
Gallery, p. 188 (top); Hans Schwarz, p. 118 (foot);
The Tate Gallery, London, pp. 53, 62, 129, 181
© DACS, 193; Valerie Thornton, p. 185;
Reproduced by kind permission of the Trustees of
the Victoria and Albert Museum, London, pp. 117
(top), 171; The Wyeth Collection © Andrew Wyeth,
p. 118 (top).

The equipment on pp. 18-20, 22, 76-84, 132-45 and
187 was kindly loaned by C J Graphic Supplies,
35-39 Old Street, London EC1 and 2-3 Great
Pulteney Street, London W1, and Daler-Rowney,
12 Percy Street, London W1.

Thanks to Stephen Mansfield for testing the drawing
projects, Richmond College of Adult Education for
testing the watercolour and oils projects, and
Kenneth Dear for testing the composition and
perspective exercises.